THE BEST OF PRIVATE EYE
1991 — 1993

ALSO AVAILABLE FROM PRIVATE EYE • CORGI

The 2nd Secret
DIARY OF JOHN MAJOR

In the second instalment of his not inconsiderably
Secret Diary, John Major again takes us
behind the scenes of the great adventure
known as Majorism
£4.99

CUTTING HUMOUR

Another Bumper Collection of Boobs
and Misprints from the World's Press
1985 — 1993
£4.99

Published in Great Britain
by Private Eye Productions Ltd
6 Carlisle Street, London W1V 5RG
in association with Corgi Books

©1993 Pressdram Ltd
ISBN 0 552 14178 x

Designed by Bridget Tisdall
Cover illustration by John Kent
Printed in England by
Clays Ltd, St Ives plc
Corgi Books are published by Transworld Publishers Ltd
61–63 Uxbridge Road, Ealing, London W5 5SA
in Australia by Transworld Publishers (Australia) Pty, Ltd
15–23 Helles Avenue, Moorebank, NSW 2170
and in New Zealand by Transworld Publishers (N.Z.) Ltd
3 William Pickering Drive, Albany, Auckland.

A GNOME IN PROVENCE

Peter Maylionaire

THE BEST OF PRIVATE EYE 1991–93
EDITED BY IAN HISLOP

PRIVATE EYE • CORGI

A Year in Advertising

by Pierre Maille

PIERRE MAILLE is a peasant from Provence. A year ago he decided to sell up his farmhouse and join an advertising agency in London. His warm and witty book tells the story of how Pierre adapts himself to his new environment.

As the pace of life slows down, this typical Frenchman begins to feel more and more relaxed. Quickly discarding his beret and clogs for the Paul Smith suit and the shirt without a tie, Pierre discovers a new world. He writes of the glorious lunches:

"Le dejeneur est magnifique. Il commence à midi and lasts until le soir. Mon favourite petit restaurant is dans Charlotte Street, where nous mangeons *outside* sur le pavement."

With Pierre as our guide, we meet a host of fascinating characters whom we soon get to know as friends.

Dave Hargleby, senior account executive on the Vidal Sassoon "Wash And Go" shampoo campaign. Chris Bogle, bow-tied creative hotshot responsible for the award-winning slogan: "Wash and go. You just wash and go. That's all there is to it. Wash and go. You see? Like the name. You wash your hair and then you go."

And then there's Simon Pratt, the media buyer who brought the "Wash And Go" campaign right into the mainstream of British life with his amazing discount rate package.

It's all here. Les meetings, les mobile phones, les bouteilles de champagne "on the client".

Pierre gloriously brings this sleepy world to life. For those who have often dreamed of loafing around in an office full of pot-plants, this is the next best thing.

As Pierre so aptly says as he sits sipping cocktails at his desk in Groucho's:

"Après le harsh world de Provence, cette advertising lark is un morçeau de gateau."

Soon to be another boring book! Le Snipcock Et Le Tweed, 28 francs.

KINNOCK A GAY MASS MURDERER

Poll Blow To Labour Hopes

by Our Mail Staff PETER VOTE-TORY

IF IT were to be revealed that Neil Kinnock was a homosexual mass-murderer in the style of Denis Nielsen, this could cost Labour the next general election.

This was the shock finding of a poll specially commissioned by the *Daily Express* from the TORI (Those Outrageous Ridiculous Idiots) organisation, which showed that 97% of the electorate would be "less likely to vote Labour" if these allegations were proved to be true.

This was the question that was put to a cross-section of over four people in our office late last night:

"If you had the choice between writing this absurd piece of Tory propaganda and being fired, which would you choose?"

74% said: "Paddy Ashdown", 12% said: "David Owen" and 25% replied: "Shorry, I've jusht been in a very important editorial conferrensh."

Major Wonderful

In a further poll, conducted next weekend, when voters were asked: "If Winnie Kinnock was found guilty of murdering four black youths with rubber necklaces, don't you think Norman Lamont is doing a brilliant job in getting inflation under control?" 100% replied: "John Major is the greatest and most statesmanlike figure in the history of politics."

The Sun-Today poll last night plunged Labour Party headquarters into a frenzy of suicidal internecine turmoil. Party members openly ran round corridors shouting: "The Tories are going to win — they're much better than us."

An anonymous leading member of the Shadow Cabinet (John Smith) said last night: "This only goes to prove that under Neil Kinnock's leadership we are all doomed — do you hear me, doomed!"

Kinnock U-turn on capital punishment

by Our Political Staff,
Peter Stringemupfellow and Hugh Trevor-Rope

"**H**ANGING'S too good for them." That was the message yesterday from Neil Kinnock as he won a standing ovation from his PR consultants after a rousing speech over the brandy and cigars in the Garrick Club.

Said Mr Kinnock: "After a long and intensive policy review, based on a study of opinion polls carried out in conjunction with the *Sun* newspaper, I have concluded that there is only one language these people understand."

Said former Socialist Kinnock (Cab No. 4273): "I mean, stands to reason, dunnit? It's a deterrent, innit? They do it to you, you've got to be prepared to give them their own medicine back.

"I mean, who'd vote Labour? You'd end up with the whole country like Liverpool. See that *GBH* on the telly? That's what it'd be like. I had that Alan Bleasdale at a fund-raising dinner at a swanky hotel once."

NEXT WEEK: Gerry Kaufmann (Cab No. 732) reviews the Labour Party's immigration policy, with special reference to sending the blacks back home.

Brixton IRA escape – that Home Office Inquiry in full

1. **The present Home Office policy is to keep innocent Irish people in jail and to let guilty ones escape.**

2. **The Inquiry feels it might be a good idea to reverse this policy.**

3. **Er…**

4. **That's it.**

ACTUALLY, I'M A CHAT SHOW HOST

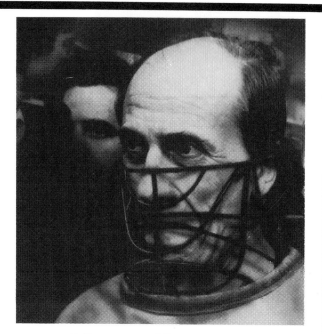

COURT CIRCULAR

BUCKINGHAM PALACE
HM the Queen flew to Hertfordshire in an aircraft of the Queen's Flight to open the new Watford Library of Computing. She was welcomed by the Lord-Lieutenant of Hertfordshire and Mr Gerald Ronson, Hon. Treasurer of the Library Appeal Fund, and Mrs Ronson.

CLARENCE HOUSE
HM the Queen Mother attended a luncheon given for the Great Ormond Street Wishing Well Appeal. She was presented by the Chief Administrator to senior consultants and leading patrons of the appeal fund, including Mr and Mrs Gerald Ronson.

KENSINGTON PALACE
HRH the Princess Margaret, Countess of Snowdon, attended a Gala Performance of Verdi's *Cigaretto* at the Royal Opera House and Business Centre, Covent Garden, where she was presented to Dame Placebo Flamingo and, representing friends of the ROHBC, Mrs Gail Ronson. She was attended by her husband, Mr G. Ronson.

KENSINGTON PALACE
Their Royal Highnesses the Prince and Princess of Wales held a private luncheon to celebrate their 30th minute together this year. Among the guests were Mr William Connolly, Sir Spike Milligan and Mr and Mrs Gail Ronson.

HRH the Prince Edward today opened a new packet of teabags at the London offices of the Really Useless Prince Company, Shaftesbury Avenue. Among those taking tea were Mr Michael Winner, Miss Jennifer Seagrove and Mr and Mrs Gail Ronson.

OPEN HOUSE
Their Royal Highnesses Mr and Mrs Gerald Ronson held a garden party at one of their London residences, Dunporridge, Regents Park. Among the guests were HM the Queen, HRH the Duke of Edinburgh, HRH the Prince Andrew and the Duchess Fergiana of York, Mr "Nosher" Stibbs, Mr "Fingers" O'Flaherty, Mr "Slasher" Noggins and many other friends.

"For God's sake, don't do it, Brian!"

Your TV Tonight

T. WOGAN *(for it is he)*: Tonight I celebrate my millionth programme by interviewing perhaps the biggest female star of all time, the most famous woman in the world. Ladies and gentlemen — Madonna.

(Camera tracks away to reveal huge golden throne, surrounded by cherubim, seraphim etc in adoring poses)

WOGAN *(taking seat on small passing cloud)*: Madonna, you've been at the top now for nearly 2,000 years. Most people would agree that you are the ultimate superstar. You've got everything you have ever wanted — fame,

millions of devoted fans, you're a role model for young girls all over the world. And yet there are those who wonder whether you are trapped by this phenomenal success that you've had. I mean, would you have thought, when you were ordinary and unknown like any other kid on the block, that one day you'd have all this power, and success, and fame? So, you're liberated, and you didn't feel you had to get married when you had that much-publicised relationship with Warren Beatty *(surely 'Joseph'? Ed)* but what I really want to know is *(contd p. 94)*

Fine old civil servants not to be disbanded

by Our Defence Staff
Brigadier Harry Trumper-Smythe

HUNDREDS of battalions of civil servants are to keep their jobs in the most controversial defence review since the battle of Crecy.

There had been fears in Whitehall that many of Britain's historic civil servants might be disbanded, as the Government looks for 90 per cent savings on the defence budget.

It had, for instance, been rumoured that the 13th-37th Floor of the MoD Penpushers and Boxwallahs were to be merged with the Queen's Own Clockwatchers and Timewasters.

But yesterday the Earl Grey was flowing at MoD HQ as the news came in that these grand old regiments had been reprieved by themselves.

Said Staff Officer (Grade 7) Mr Horace Norris: "This is a great day for us. We have worn 'the Suit' with pride for 30 years, and many of us have given our whole lives to the Service. We didn't fight to get a seat on the 8.05 from Haywards Heath just to see a lot of useless soldiers keeping their jobs."

Red Tape Brigade

The Queen was reported to be taking "a close personal interest" in the future of her unarmed forces. A Buckingham Palace spokesman said: "Thanks to these imaginative cuts, we still have the largest and most professional army of civil servants in the world. It is just a pity that all the soldiers, sailors and airmen had to go."

Radio Programmes and how not to listen to them

with John Cleese and Dr Robyn Beard

CLEESE: Hullo everyone. Today we're going to talk about anger in the listener-radio context.

BEARD: Yes, this is quite a common syndrome.

CLEESE: What happens exactly?

BEARD: Well, take a programme where two men — they could be pretty dull — drone on about family life — the tension and so forth.

CLEESE: That could make you pretty angry, could it?

BEARD: It could indeed.

CLEESE: And then we bottle up our anger, do we?

BEARD: Some do, some don't. It depends a lot on your psychological makeup.

CLEESE: You once told me in one of our therapy sessions, when you feel the pressure building up, to pick up the radio and throw it out of the window.

"I wish that bloody Thesaurus would shut up!"

BEARD: I remember it well. It helps to let off steam.

CLEESE: And get rid of your old steam radio. Ha ha ha!

BEARD: Ha ha ha!

CLEESE: Next week — how to cope with endless *Monty Python* repeats on the telly.

It's Your Line to Fragrant Mary

FIRST CALLER: Hullo Mary, it's Jasper from Esher. We met when Jeffrey came down to do our AGM last year. Look, it's not easy for me to discuss this, but there's this friend of mine — yes, let's just call him my friend — who's got himself into a spot of bother with this Lloyd's business.

MRS MARY ARCHER *(putting on ghastly soft caring voice):* Oh, I am sorry. Do go on. It helps to talk to someone.

CALLER: Yes, well it all began when I — I mean my friend — met this broker chap a few years ago, and he said: "Look, it's money for old rope. You sign on to become a Name, and then every year we send you a cheque. Sometimes it might just be £20,000. In a good year it could be a million."

MARY THATCHER: And then what happened?

CALLER: Well, Mary, everything went swimmingly until a couple of months ago, when one morning I had this note to say that I owed them £50 million, and they wanted it by return.

MARY ARCHER: You're not alone, love, it's a very common problem. I suppose you had to sell the house, and the Jag and the yacht and the Renoir, and take your kids out of school, right?

CALLER: Oh no, I just hopped it to Bermuda. Or rather my friend did. But what I want to know, Mary, is — could you come out here for dinner? I'll send my jet.

MARY: Next distressed caller please.

SECOND CALLER: Hullo, Mrs Archer. You remember me from the trial? I was the one in the wig who really fancied you like mad! I can still remember the exotic scent of your perfume wafting through the court and driving all us lawyers wild with lust *(pant pant)*.

MRS ARCHER: Get off the line before I have you arrested...

Ring Fragrant Mary now if you've lost all your money at Lloyd's — 0868 211777 (£25,000 a minute peak rate. Adult idiots only)

TENTH ANNIVERSARY

Let's have dinner alone

Good idea. You stay here. I'll go to Scotland

'Peregrine Worsthorne will never kick sand in my face again!' says Andrew Neill

Are you fed up with being bullied by snobs? Are you sick of Alexander Chancellor being rude to you or Dominic Lawson not asking you to lunch? Do you envy A.N. Wilson his glamorous lifestyle and does Charles Moore's success with the girls make you jealous? Has Henry Porter looked down his nose at you lately?

I know how you feel!! But now, with my amazing Two-Stage Anti-Snob Home Course *you too* can triumph over the snobbocracy!!

Here's how it works:

■ **Stage One: Become Editor of the** *Sunday Times.*

■ **Stage Two: Write a piece in the Style Section headed: "Why Don't I Get Invited To More Parties With Posh Upper-Class Birds?"**

I guarantee that within MINUTES the snobs will be on the run, defeated, destroyed and devastated by your amazing powers of confidence.

It worked for me!!

Simply fill in this form and send at once to the *Sunday Times*.

Please rush me the Andrew Neill Two-Stage Anti-Snob Home Course at once. (£3.10)
I am over 18 and rather sad.

Name . . . .

Address . . . .

. . . .

. . . .

TV HIGHLIGHTS

I Love Lucy

Channel 4 (black and white)

Repeat of the hilarious sitcom set in America where an elderly couple go on honey moon and then tell everyone about it in the Sunday Telegraph. Lucy is the zany comedienne Lady Lucinda Lambton, whose offbeat sense of humour is perfectly matched by the whacky antics of Sir Peregrine Worsthorne.

In tonight's episode, Lucy falls in love with an old antique (Perry) and marries him. They fly off to America on a romantic freebie (courtesy of Delta Airline's Legover Special) and end up in the middle of the Grand Canyon. The fun begins when Perry and Lucy start arguing. Is his article worse than her photographs? Or are her photographs worse than his article? It's one of those quarrels that are bound to end in tears. Of boredom. From readers of the Sunday Telegraph

Eye rating: Z-z-z-z-z-z

ITN (AND ALL OTHER CHANNELS)

The dramatic moment you missed during the commercial break

THE SUN SAYS

We Salute John Mc-Carthy. A Hero For Our Times

His example has inspired the world. His courage, his fortitude and his good humour in adversity. It was a display of British spirit at its very best. It makes us all proud.

The *Sun* says:

When are you going to get your leg over, John?

TREVOR BARBADOS: ...and it seems that John McCarthy's plane hasn't arrived yet here at RAF Lyneham, but of course as soon as it does we'll be bringing you news. Unfortunately this means that we can't yet ask him directly how he feels at the moment, but on the line from Sweden we've got Professor Lündblom of Malmo University who has made a special study of the psychology of hostage-release. Professor, how do you think John McCarthy will be feeling at this moment? Will he be feeling exhilarated or depressed?

PROFESSOR: ...er...

BARBADOS: ...or will he be feeling a mixture of them both?

PROFESSOR: Well, the hostage who is undergoing the trauma of release is likely to be experiencing conflicting emotions. On the one hand, he is very pleased to be free. On the other hand, as he looks out at all those interviewers waiting to ask him how he feels, he may well experience profound feelings of depression...

BARBADOS: I'm sorry, Professor, we'll have to stop you there because the plane still hasn't landed here... er... in the meantime we've now got Michael Hack on the line from Damascus. Michael, you've actually asked John McCarthy how he felt. How did you feel in putting that question?

HACK: ...er...

BARBADOS: You feel elated, or depressed — or a mixture of both?

HACK: Well, Trevor, the mood here in Damascus is one of intense excitement, mingled, it has to be said, with a certain depression. Syrian Foreign Ministry sources were saying this morning...

BARBADOS: I'm sorry, Michael, we've got to break off there, because there's a report in that the plane definitely hasn't landed so... er... I've got a relative here — my cousin, who has been very close to me while I've been covering the hostage situation over the past five years. What's the mood tonight amongst my family as they see me on the television asking people how they feel?

MAN HOLDING CANDLE: Well, we were elated, obviously, but let us not forget all those people who haven't been on television being asked how they felt...

BARBADOS: I'm sorry, we're going to have to cut you off there, to go straight back to the airport, where I understand that nothing is happening. David, can you confirm that nothing is happening?

REPORTER: Yes, Peter, I can confirm that the mood here at the airfield is one of intense anticipation. We're still waiting for something to happen.

BARBADOS: How do you feel about that? Would you say that you are depressed, or elated, or a mixture of...

(Cont. round the clock on all channels)

"Are you sure you wouldn't like us to provide a partner?"

EXCLUSIVE TO ALL NEWSPAPERS

The Undiscovered Joys of
FRIBI

by **Our Travel Correspondent**

THE ISLAND of Fribi lies like a jewel in the azure Mediterranean Sea off the wooded coast of Manturia. It was here that the ancient Romans built their temple to the Goddess Frilodia in 346 BC and it was here that the British Airways 787 landed over 12 centuries later after a short and comfortable journey with an inflight meal consisting of the following delicious items: A Pomerade of Poulet Froid avec Lettuce Manquis; A Tranche of Home-Cured Jambon Bernard Mathieu (sell-by date July 91); Gateau de Lord King; A Demi-Bouteille of Vin de Boeing 1991.

Fribi has much to offer the serious traveller, including a particularly fine walk around the harbour (where once Byron stayed as a guest of the Comtessa Legovia), which leads naturally to the restaurant of Signor Chancellori and his beautiful wife Peregrina. Here, for as little as nothing at all, I ate a wonderful meal consisting of the following items: Ragatino di Frutti di Mare *(That's enough food. Ed)*.

The local people believe that the ancient spring which bubbles up under the olive groves of Fribi's hinterland was the very one that Napoleon drank from following his defeat at the Battle of Sessione in 1804. Certainly Alfredo, who has run the gift shop

there (Alfredo's Gift Shop) since 1979, believes the legend and in his shop you can purchase all manner of Napoleonic and other souvenirs. These are all made by local *artisones* and include: a plastic replica of the earthenware cup used by the Emperor; a set of leather coasters showing views of Oxford Colleges *(shurely 'the island of Fribi'? Ed)*; a packet of car stickers saying FRIBIANS DO IT FOR NOTHING; t-shirts bearing the legend MADE IN TAIWAN.

When you've had your fill of the delights of Fribian shopping at Alfredo's then there is always the beach and "Johnny's Surf Bar", run by the enterprising Australian Studley Bruce Palling, who "came over for a holiday and decided to stay". You can rent or buy from Studley a marvellous range of windsurfing and scuba-diving gear and he will even teach you Hydroparaski-diving at a very reasonable rate.

Then it's back to the hotel (and it has to be the Fribi Ramada, with its glorious pool, light airy rooms, underground disco and beauty salon) for a cocktail.

In the Salmonella Bar, ask for Hans and he will rustle you up his famous Nuremburg Stinger.

What a perfect end to a day!

Yes, Fribi is the most perfect unspoilt holiday paradise that I have stayed in since last week.

● *Our Correspondent travelled to Fribi with GnomeSun Holiday Tours on a Special 7-Night Breakaway Special Break. He flew British Airways Club Executive Diamond Class to Pavarotti Airport and hired a Fiat Uno from Fribi Rental Co. His travel insurance came from Gnome AllCover plc.*

The cost of his trip in total came to: £0.00p.

"…the women come and go, talking of Michelangelo…"

The five lost years of John McCarthy

by Our Fillinguploadsofthepaperwhileeveryoneisaway Staff

IT SEEMS incredible, but the shy figure who stepped smiling into his new freedom is entirely oblivious of the world-shattering events of the last five years.

He has missed:

● The wedding of Sir Peregrine Worsthorne and his blushing bride Lady Lucinda Lamppost.

● Gazza's video of *Fog on the Tyne*.

● Michael Ignatieff appointed columnist on the *Observer*.

● The introduction of the new 5p piece by John Major.

● The film *Batman* starring Jerry Hall.

● The *Hello* special edition, featuring the Duke & Duchess of York's new home.

● The new British Telecom logo — it will mean nothing to John.

● The libel action between Count Nikolai Tolstoy and Lord Aldington.

● The launch and closure of the *Sunday Correspondent*.

● The marriage of Lucinda Lambchop and Sir Peregrine *(You're fired. Ed)*

(continued on all channels)

TREVOR BARBADOS: ...and we've just got news of something happening now in Moscow, so we'll go over to Penny Marshall in the Honeymoon Suite of the Legova Hotel, who is only two miles from the Russian Parliament building, where we're expecting something to happen at any minute.

(Still photograph of gorgeous, pouting ITN hackette holding telephone)

PENNY: Stop it, Tim, give over, I'm on *News At Ten*. Yes, Trevor, what was it you wanted to know?

BARBADOS *(reading from autocue)*: What's the latest there, Penny?

PENNY: Well, a few minutes ago it was very quiet. But before that I definitely heard the sound of gunfire. At least I think it was gunfire, it may have been thunder.

BARBADOS: Could it have been gunfire?

PENNY: It's very quiet here at the moment, Trevor.

BARBADOS: Thank you, Penny, we'll be back to you the minute nothing happens. And now over to the BBC, to see if they know what's happening.

(Switches on television in front of him on his ridiculous desk)

JOHN SIMPSON *(for it is he, standing in BBC studio in Moscow in front of picture of tank)*: ... so it's almost impossible to say what's happening at all. There are rumours flying around in all directions — 3,000 tanks are about to attack Boris Yeltsin's Parliament building, the entire KGB has had a heart attack, and there is an unconfirmed report from the Legova Hotel that there has been some kind of an earth tremor in Room 1317 — but, quite honestly, none of us have the slightest idea what's going on, particularly me since I only arrived in Moscow twenty minutes ago. Back to the studio.

DAVID DIMBLEBY: Thank you, John, and since nothing seems to be happening, we've got some Russians into the studio... *(Camera pans to three hastily assembled Russians)* ... Mr Yuri Timefillev, who is *(reads from script)* a member of the Ukrainian House of Deputies, Mr Anatoly Wafflov, the London correspondent of *Moscow and Moscowmen*, the outspoken economic quarterly, and Mr Dmitri McGonagallov, the well-known Kazakh poet. But, before we talk to any of them, we've got an interview which Martin Sixminutes was lucky enough to be given in 1987 with the man who is Mr Gorbachev's successor as President of the Soviet Union, Mr Cantrememberhisnameov. This is a huge scoop because it gives a unique insight into the thinking of the man who may well be running the Soviet Union for many hours to come.

(Film of grey-faced man behind desk talking in Russian. Silly translator's voice over)

"... and that is why I am totally dedicated to the goals of glasnost and perestroika and 100 per cent loyal to Mikhail Sergeyvitch Gorbachev, the democratically elected Supreme President of Soviet Praesidium and General Secretary of Communist Party of Soviet..."

SIXPACK *(in Russian)*: Z-z-z-z-z... *(Translator: Zh-zh-zh-zh...)*

(Cut back to Barbados watching screen)

BARBADOS: Well there doesn't seem to be anything happening on BBC1. Let's go over live now to *Newsnight*...

(Switches channel)

PETER SNOW *(standing in front of sandpit with hastily built cardboard model of Russian Parliament building where Baghdad used to be)*: ... so the elite Republican Guard seemed to have moved up — that's the Soviet Republican Guard, not the Russian Republican Guard — and they really are crack troops, whose loyalty to the Kremlin is beyond question. Isn't that right, Rear-Admiral Sir Fitzroy-Bogus?

(Cut to woman in tweed suit, with caption reading BORIS YELTSIN)

WOMAN: No, Peter, as I explained to Sue MacGregor on the *Today* programme this morning, and again on *World At One*, the 103rd Republican Guard Paratroop Regiment defected yesterday to the Russian officers of the KGB.

SNOW: That's the Soviet officers of the Russian KGB, you mean?

WOMAN: No, I mean the Russian officers of the Soviet KGB loyal to General Demokratoff, who is Boris Yeltsin's Vice-President...

SNOW: I must cut you short there, because we've got Kate Adie on the line from Tallinn and she's absolutely furious because she's got

landed somewhere where nothing seems to be happening.

(Still of Kate Adie in battle-fatigues standing next to tank in desert. Caption reads SUE MACGREGOR)

MacGREGOR: Well, I think the one question we all want an answer to this morning — I know I do — is what is going to be the response from the Central Asian republics like Uzbekistan? Are they going to declare their colours by coming out behind Boris Yeltsin, or are they going to bide their time by waiting to see which way the wind blows? I have with me in the studio Brian Redhead, who is an expert in everything. Brian, before I ask you about the all-important Tadzhik question, could we have the sports news from Mark Dull?

DULL: Yes, Sue, the main news this morning is that Neasden's big new six-figure signing from Tbilisi Magneto, Yuri Kickoff, may not now be in the number five shirt in time for next Tuesday's Ryman's Charity Shield away-leg needle-match against Dollis Hill.

BRIAN BIGHEAD: I'm sorry, we've got to interrupt the sports news there for a very important time-check. It's now time for me to ask a very very long question to my guest, the distinguished Kremlin-watcher Dr Anatoly Izvestia of St Ignoramus's College, Oxford, so that I can show that I know a lot more about Russia than he does.

SUE MacGREGOR: That won't be hard.

IZVESTIA: Can I just explain at this point that we experts are almost certain now that there has been some sort of coup, probably triggered by dissatisfaction at Mr Gorbachev's handling of the Soviet economy and it now seems certain that Gorbachev is finished forever...

(Cut back to Peter Snow)

SNOW *(still by sandtable)*: And it really does seem now as though something very unpleasant is going to happen at last. There are guns going off, tanks rolling in, crowds building up, every kind of indication that hundreds of people are going to be killed at any moment. So let's just remind ourselves of the situation on the ground.

(Snow runs over to sandtable and begins to wave arms about and foam at mouth)

SNOW: Now, here in the middle we have the famous White House. It's not *the* White House, of course. Nor is it white. Nor is it a house. But it's where Boris Hussein has got his nerve-centre. He's probably even now, as the allied tanks close in, here, and here, and here, hiding in his bunker millions of miles below the ground, waiting for the final assault. *(Bangs on sandpit)* Boris, are you there? Can you hear me?

(Enter uninvited "expert" in shape of corpulent media magnate)

R. MAXWELL *(for it is he)*: Let me make one thing perfectly clear to you, Mr Snow. I've got very good contacts in the Kremlin indeed. All the top men are personal friends of mine, especially this new chap who's taken over, can't remember his name for the moment. I've been on the line to Moscow in the last few minutes, and I can tell you that Boris Yeltsin is almost certainly dead.

(Screen shows Yeltsin addressing 2 million people in front of White House, captioned LIVE FROM MOSCOW)

YELTSIN *(for it is he)*: Hullo Bob, hullo Trevor, hullo Peter, hullo Penny. This is your old friend Boris, alive and well, waiting for something to happen.

TREVOR BARBADOS: I must just interrupt you there, Boris, as I believe that something is happening at the Legova Hotel. Penny Marshall? Is something happening?

PENNY: Yes, yes, yes...

ANNOUNCER: We interrupt this programme to bring you some news. We're terribly sorry, but the coup's over.

A KGB Doctor writes

As a KGB doctor I am often telling people they are ill.

To the layman they appear perfectly healthy, and in full possession of all their faculties.

But to the expert eye, such as mine, it will be clear at once that they are suffering from *Perestroikitis normalis* or severe Glasnost and are therefore in need of a violent purge.

If you are feeling well, you should avoid your doctor at all cost.

© *A Doctor*

'I know just how Mr Gorbachev feels'

An exclusive interview with the **Rt Hon Mrs Margaret** Thatcher, ex-Supreme Ruler of the Universe, by her devoted admirer, TV's **Charles Moore.**

"How wonderful of you to call."

A S SOON as I heard the awful news about this ghastly coup in Russia, and the overthrow of Mr Gorbachev, I knew there was only one person in London I wanted to talk to.

Fortunately, just at that moment, the telephone rang and it was her.

"Prime Minister," I said.

"Shut up Moore and get out your notebook," she intervened, in those imperious tones that once made the world seem so safe and reassuring.

"One knows just how poor Mr Gorbachev must be feeling at this moment," she dictated. "A towering world figure, a statesman with vision, stabbed treacherously in the back by pygmies, whom she herself had appointed."

"Surely you mean..." I began.

"Be quiet! I haven't finished," she continued. "One minute one is standing alone at the helm of the ship of state, carrying on one's shoulders all the awesome responsibility of pushing a tremendous revolution that is going to reshape the world — the free market, democracy, privatisation, poll tax. And then what happens? Suddenly, when one is out of the country, they come out from the woodwork — the faceless grey little men with their tidy bureaucratic minds — and everything one has striven for is overturned in a moment."

By this time, listening to the greatest leader in the western world, I was in tears.

"I can see it all," she went on. "I've been there myself. I too know what it is to hear the knock on the door in the middle of the night, and see the faceless men who owe their whole careers to me, standing there having the barefaced audacity to tell me that one was no longer fit to run the country, that one's great revolution had failed, that one would have to stand down.

"And you know, Mr Moore, what really hurts," she continued, "is that these were Mikhail's closest colleagues. Men like John Major, Norman Lamontov and all those others whose names I can't remember. How dare they ..."

At this moment she broke off, and I heard in the background the television news announcing that the coup was over.

"Did you hear that, Charles?" she screamed. "The nightmare is over. The plotters have admitted defeat. They've brought her back! I'm on my way to the Kremlin now. My people are out in the streets to welcome me..."

© A Mooretrash/Daily Hellograph Production

For God's sake, leave them alone!

says Glenda Slagg in the village of L'Aigue-aux-Verres, Provence

J ILL MORRELL and John McCarthy are just another couple in love. For years they have been waiting for this moment of happiness when they can look into each other's eyes, smile and rekindle their love for each other away from the prying eyes of the world.

How sickening, then, to find that the prurient media have tracked them down to this tiny cottage in France. It should have been their dream holiday, but it has now turned into a nightmare! How loathsome of the peeping paparazzi to hound John 'n' Jill in their well-deserved days of wine and roses.

"Are the press being intrusive?" I shouted through the letterbox as I shoved a microphone into the hallway.

"Aren't you sick of the tabloids?" I asked as I climbed up the ivy and tried to force my way in through an upstairs window.

"Do you want to be alone?" I screamed through the keyhole of the bedroom into which they had locked themselves.

Their reply was sadly drowned out by the sound of the helicopter lowering my photographer down the chimney. However his pictures tell the poignant story of two young lovers who just want some time to themselves.

Why oh why can't anyone get the message?

© Glenda Slagg

NEXT WEEK: Are they at it? An exclusive report.

"Not pastor again!"

YOUNG EYE

The new Russia — your guide to the new nations emerging from the Soviet shadow.

RUSSIA

Formerly the Soviet Union, occupying half the world's land surface. Now an independent country occupying half the world's TV coverage. Main export: people.

ESTHERRANTZONIA

Formerly Republic of Leninia. Occupied by Stalin in 1933. Capital: Thatslith (formerly Stallinn). Chief import: Kate Adie.

KACHATURIAN

Little-known Central Asian republic, formerly Stalinastan. Populated by nomadic cameramen making films for BBC2 entitled *Kachaturian — The Unknown Land That The World Forgot*.

GAZZASTAN

Football-crazy Moslem republic somewhere down at the bottom on the right. Little is known about this new country in the Young Eye office.

VODKASTAN

Drink-crazed republic somewhere under table. Capital: Jeffbinin (formerly Smirnoff).

IMRANKHAN

Cricket-mad, sex-crazed, Moslem *(That's enough, Republics. Ed.)*

Joint Apology
Mr Boris Yeltsin and
Mr Mikhail Gorbachev

We, in common with all other newspapers in the West during the last five years, may have given the impression that we believed Mr Mikhail Gorbachev to be the saviour of his people, a man of superhuman abilities and the only person capable of leading the Soviet Union into the twentieth century; whilst Mr Boris Yeltsin was described as "a drunken rabble rouser", "a loony demagogue" and "a Fascist".

We now realise that throughout our coverage, due to a printing error, the names of these two men were invariably transposed.

We, of course, meant to say that Mr Boris Yeltsin was a towering statesman, a man of courage and destiny and the only figure capable of leading his country from the shackles of the past to the light of democracy.

At the same time, Mr Gorbachev should have been described as "a bungling bureaucrat, hopelessly incapable of delivering his promises and an out-of-step reactionary fascist to boot".

We apologise to both gentlemen for any distress that this regrettable technical error may have caused.

THOSE SIMPSONS IN FULL

John Simpson, BBC's popular Diplomatic Editor. The grey-haired sexpot who watched a cruise missile flying past his bedroom window in Baghdad. Author of book *Wow! Look What's Going Past My Bedroom Window in Baghdad*.

Bob Simpson, the BBC's popular Baghdad Correspondent. His authoritative reports on the *Today* programme kept the nation sane during the dark days of the Gulf War. Not to be confused with...

John Timpson, BBC's popular radio presenter. The grey-haired sexpot was formerly star of Radio Four's *Today* programme.

Bart Simpson, popular Sky comic character, famous for ridiculous catchphrases such as "Buy My T-shirt" and "Win A Sky Dish".

Simpson's of Piccadilly, elderly shop with knock-down cashmere sweaters (sale price: £799.99).

John Simpson, architect best known for design of Paternoster Square rejected by Prince Charles.

Mrs Simpson, American heiress and wife of Edward Fox, the *Daily Telegraph*'s award-winning defence correspondent.

Anthony Simpson, famous author of *Anatomy of Victoria Brittain*, a rude pop-up book featuring the famous left-wing sexpot.

Bill Simpson, greyhaired star of TV's long-running Scottish soap opera *Dr Simpson's Casebook*. Well known for his catchphrase "Mine's a large Scotch, Janet."

N.F. Simpson, famous right-wing playwright and *(That's enough Simpsons. Ed.)*

Neasden Satanic Abuse hearing continues

Day 94

THE examination-in-chief continued today of Mr Kevin Spart, Director of the Neasden Social Services Child Care Outreach Snatch Squad.

Mr Spart told the court that the children of families X, B, Z, F and Q all told remarkably similar stories relating to an incident alleged to have taken place last December at St Eggwith's Church of England Primary School in Tesco Road, Neasden.

The Reverend 'P' was clearly identified by the witnesses as the organiser of a bizarre ritual centred on the effigy of a baby. Children described how they had been made by the Reverend 'P' to dress up in flimsy costumes, some so skimpy that their lower limbs were visible. Others had clumsy cardboard "wings" fitted to their backs. A live sheep was introduced into the proceedings, Mr Spart told the hearing, and three of the children were "dressed up" by the Reverend 'P's' wife in "adult clothing", including false beards, turbans and "crowns". These three children, described as J, M and D, told of "offering gifts" to the effigy, including various sweet-smelling, oriental drug-like substances. Shepherds' crooks also played some undefined part in the ritual, it was alleged.

At the climax of the ceremony, the Reverend 'P' led the children in a ritual dance, singing the words "Awa ina manja", which were almost certainly taken from a satanic black mass.

Mr Spart said that in view of the "overwhelming nature" of the evidence he had had no alternative but to order the slaughter of all the first-born of Neasden.

The hearing continues.

"Hi, what's your name, Happy Birthday, I love you, let's have children, goodbye"

Disney Royal Row Shock

by Our Court Staff The *Observer's* **Donald Duckford**

THE WALT Disney Corporation announced yesterday that it was with deep regret that it had issued instructions to Mr Michael Mouse, the veteran Hollywood star, that he was on no account to be photographed with the so-called "Duchess of York".

Said a Disney spokesman: "Fergiana is a ridiculous cartoon character, whose absurd antics, silly clothes and tasteless jokes would be totally out of keeping with the dignity of the Disney family. Furthermore, we think it likely that the Duchess would attempt to use the photo opportunity for commercial purposes: for example, to promote her books and other merchandising or to get herself into *Hello* magazine."

A Palace spokesman was unavailable for comment last night.

TV Tonight
Edinburgh Nightzzzzzz

Tonight Tracy Wargs looks at the highlights of another week at the Edinburgh Festival and Fringe. Includes:

● The Kurdish Jazz Octet. Cool jazz from the northern borders of Iraq. Newly formed combo plays works by Monk, Parker, and Madonna.

● *Stuff yer Poll Tax, Thatch!* from the Street Theatre of Inverness. An improvised play starring Murray Spart and Rory McSpart directed by Ken McLoach.

● *Two Men in Bow Ties Making Camp Jokes.* Insiders predict that these two ex-Canterbury choirboys (Jamie Twist and Tristram Milkfloat) are definitely

Late night at the Traverse: Julian Critchley

the next Kit and the Widow (*Who they? Ed.*)

● *Mother Albania Weeps* by the legendary Mzslpzghh Theatre of Mime. Ten hours long, this new translation into Italian by Umberto Woosta has stunned audiences throughout Europe.

● Exhibition of post-glasnost satirical ceramics including works by Stodoffski, Scarvovitch and Nikolai Garlandov. *(That's enough Edinburgh. Ed.)*

The Daily Hellograph

FINAL

ESTABLISHED 1855 NO. 42,339

40p

LONDON AND MANCHESTER

FRIDAY, JANUARY 17, 1992

Patricia Hodge admits 'I'm amazed'

By Our Political, Economic and Current Affairs Staff

A DELIGHTED Patricia Hodge *(Who she? Ed)* told the *Daily Hellograph* last night that she was delighted, at the age of 45, to have been put on the front page of the best-selling quality daily newspaper.

"It is a miracle," she said in a heartwarming interview given only to the *Daily Hellograph* and the other tabloids.

"To be honest," she said, fighting back the reporters *(shurely 'tears'? Ed).* "I only ever expected to have a little story on the inside page of the *Express* or possibly *Today*. But when the doctors told me that I

had delivered a huge front page photo story to a serious newspaper I was lost for words."

The father of the story, *Hellograph* reporter James Dellingpole, said that he too was "gobsmacked" by the sheer size of the picture.

"It is terrific news," he said. "Or rather it isn't news at all. Nature is wonderful. A few days ago the Hodge baby was little more than an agent's handout in a filing tray marked IF YOU'RE DESPERATE FOR A FILLER. And yesterday it knocked Russia and its starving millions right off the front page."

Hodge baby silent on Hellograph shocker

By Our Foreign, Home, Social and Sports Staff

PATRICIA Hodge's newly born baby, provisionally named Max Hastings Dellingpole Moore Hodge, has refused to comment on his mother's surprise appearance on the front page of the world's greatest newspaper.

Wearing an all-in-one romper suit, the baby remained tight-lipped during an exclusive and heartwarming interview with the *Daily Hellograph*.

When asked if he had any views on why his mother should

appear in a total non-story all over the *Hellograph*'s front page, he smiled enigmatically and went back to sleep.

Patricia Hodge is 45.

"Have you seen the photo of Patricia Hodge on the front page of the Hellograph?"

Hellograph owner to bed Sunday Times dish

(shurely 'wed Sunday Times award-winning columnist'? Ed)

By Our Media Staff Jane Thynne-Stuff

THE PROPRIETOR of the *Daily Hellograph*, Sir Conrad Blackadder, today announced his forthcoming enslavement to the heartwarming charms of top Canadian model Barbara Amiel.

Said Sir Blackadder: "This is the sort of up-beat happy story that should go on the front page of the *Hellograph*."

Barbara Amiel is 56-26-36.

WEATHER

Sunny, Heartwarming
Details — Back Page

ON OTHER PAGES

DOCTOR ON THE JOB

I SHALL never forget the day I met Roy Jenkins. It was on a rainy day in Westminster and I saw a lonely figure standing drinking a large glass of claret on the terrace. There was a full moon and across the river the lights twinkled in Jeffrey Archer's penthouse.

I had never believed in love at first sight, but this was the reality at this electric moment. I went home and wrote him a poem.

The stars shone at our
meeting, Woy.
I knew at once that you were
my boy.
"Labour's drift to the left has
to be stopped."
When you said this my eyes
popped.

I WAS always jealous of Shirley Williams. With her immaculate hair and fabulous dress sense, she seemed to exercise a mystical power over him. It was always Shirley this, Shirley that. I felt so upset I wrote another poem and sent it to Roy.

If I ever hate any girlie
It has to be that awful
Shirley.
What do you see in her, Roy?
I weep.
As for William Rogers, he's a
creep.

I PUT my whole heart and soul into these poems. Later, when the Gang of Four was announced, I wrote the following poem, which is probably my masterpiece:

Tea for two, and two for tea.
Me for Woy, and Woy for me.
Let us dump this Gang of
Four,
The other two are terrific
bore(s).

Soon to be a major drama-documentary from Granada.

CAST

David Owen	DIRK BOGARDE
Roy Jenkins	ROY KINNEAR
Shirley Williams	PATRICIA HAYES
William Rogers	HIMSELF

"Which one of us is charismatic?"

TINDLEBURY-ON-THE-MARSH CHRISTIAN ASSOCIATION

RGJ 1991

Doctor to quit

'My genius unappreciated in Britain'

by Our Political Staff **E.N.O. Good**

THE renaissance man of British politics, Dr Jonathan Owen, has announced his decision to leave the stage and go abroad, if offered a suitably important post such as President of the World.

The doctor first rose to prominence as one of the famous "Gang of Four", who smashed the mould of British comedy with their now-legendary revue *Beyond The Labour Party*.

Pop-up everywhere

From there the doctor went from strength to strength as he staged one brilliant theatrical coup after another — the SDP, the Alliance, the Two Davids, the One David, Rosie and Me and All Washed Up.

But the critics were not always favourable, and the doctor increasingly came to feel that his superhuman talents were not being properly recognised in what he called "this piddly little tinpot backwater they call Britain".

Woy Oh Woy

But now the doctor sees a new world beckoning. What will it be? Will he return to medicine, to win a Nobel Prize? Will he succeed Perez de Worsthorne as Secretary-General of the *Sunday Telegraph* Comment Section? Or will he take off in his Tardis, to roam through time and space, to conquer new worlds?

Whatever he does, one thing is certain. We shall not look upon his like again, until he comes back.

School announcements

St Cakes

The Lonrho Term begins today. There are 1312 boys and 2 gays in the school *(shurely 'girls'? W.D.)*. A.J.P. Haagen-Dazs (Lamont's) is Senior Chairman of the Collegium. Miss Tracy Sound-Beit (Patten's) is Head of Suspenders. The Rev. B.C.C.I. Hiatus-Hernia has left to become chief executive of the First Episcopal Church of Rock 'n' Roll, Salt Lake City. His place as Chaplain is taken by Rabbi Julia Hamburger. Mr A.P.R. Nurofen has been appointed Head of Stress-Counselling and will be available to all pupils and members of staff in his study in the Du Cann Library Complex between 7 and 8 on Wednesdays. There will be no Classics Department as from this term, and Mr F.F. Joyrider will be redeployed teaching Kaifu wrestling to the Junior Shell. The Drabble Run will take place at Stringfellows on 23rd October. A performance of Puccini's *Nessun Dorma* conducted by Mr Jon Birtwistle (O.C.) will be given in the Worship Centre on 22nd November: solo tenor Justin Cornetto (Wall's). Tickets from the Bursar, Major Yazov-Smythe, Dunyeltsin, Terreblanche Crescent, Milton Keynes MK 40. The OC Lodge (477) Annual Dinner-Dance will be held in the Gorman Room of the Berni-Grant Hotel, Billericay (M25, exit 314). The Grand Weasel (Mr R.S.J. Switchcard) will preside, assisted by the Imperial Wizard of the Raspberry Ripple (Mr R.Q. Specimen-Signature). Recoveries will be in the second half of the term.

St Cake's was ranked 890th in the recent Daily Telegraph Independent Schools A-Level Performance Survey.

After months of

intense

thought our admen
couldn't come up
with any

fresh

ideas. So here is a bird
with no clothes on.

Tïtzan-Darz

You can't get your leg over her. So
buy some ice cream instead.

(continued from 6.30 a.m.)

BRIAN BIGHEAD: ... which is where we'll have to leave you, Mr Vassillynov, thank you for talking to us. That leaves just time for a final comment from you, Professor Stringvestia, and I must ask you to be brief as we only have very limited time at our disposal, one minute forty-five seconds to be precise, and the question I would like to put to you, and I must repeat, we are very short of time so could you please be as concise as possible, which in the light of today's dramatic developments, how do you see the situation in the independent republics as they move towards a sort of federal structure with power devolved from the centre to the local level. I know it is a difficult question to answer in the space of what is now twenty seconds but could you sum up in a sentence how you feel about these historic changes?

PROFESSOR: Er...

BIGHEAD: I'm sorry, I shall have to cut you off there. And now here's Brian Perkins with news of what's on Radio Four.

LUGUBRIOUS MAN WITH BEARD: Later today, a four-part four-hour special on the Trade Union Congress. We ask: "Is anyone interested in the TUC?"

That's in addition to our live coverage of today's main conference debate: "Is anyone interested in the TUC?" And this evening at 7.30 Norman Willis faces a panel of young trade unionists who ask: "Does anyone care about the unions any more?"

And finally at 10.00pm *The Beard Programme*, with Sue Barbie. Tonight's topics for discussion include new techniques for beard-trimming from Alaska; are bearded men the objects of discrimination in the office? And is there a link between beards and cancer? That's tonight's *Beard Programme* at ten.

BIGHEAD: And now over to Glasgow for the latest news on the TUC Conference...

"Click! You are now looking at your own home. You have forgotten to hand your cassette guide in at the gallery..."

GLENDA SLAGG

FLEET STREET'S OWN KERB-CRAWLER!!!

■ SERVE him right!?!? Sir Allan Dirty Mac I'm talkin' about, stoopid?!?! Director of Public Prosecutions? Depraved Pursuer of Prostitutes, more like it?!?! (Geddit?) You should be ashamed of yourself, Mr Lawman!?!? Spendin' your nights a-boozin' and a-cruisin' around the red light district?!?

What you need is a nice gal with a flat in Pimlico and a lot of time on her hands?!! Like me!!?! Mmmm... *(You're fired. Ed.)*

● SPARE a tear for poor Sir Allan, who was drummed out of office jus' 'cause he fancied a bit of slap 'n' tickle of an evening?!?! He's only human, for cryin' out loud!!? Leave him alone, Mister Humbug, and let him get on with it!?! What harm does it do, I ask you? We're not living in the Middle Ages, for heaven's sake?!? Hats off to Sir Allan!? Give 'im a knighthood?! (He's already got one. You're fired. Ed.)

■ THREE cheers for Liz Taylor?!? It's eighth time lucky for her and her new hubby Larry?!? Doesn't it warm your heart that lovely Liz who only yesterday was at death's door has today found lasting happiness in the arms of her hunky he-man?!?! There's hope for all of us!?! Pass me the Kleenex, Mister, I'm goin' to have a wee weep for Liz 'n' Larry!!!?! Boo-hoo-hoo?!!!

● COUNTESS of Finchley?! That's Mrs Thatcher's noo title, dummy! There's plenty of killjoys in the meeja who want to go round a-leerin' and a-sneerin' jus' 'cause Maggie is joining the Nobs and Nobesses in the House of Lords?!? Not me Mister!!? I reckon Our Maggie will kick some life into those moth-eaten old fogeys?!!? Good on yer, Ma'am!! Next stop Buckingham Palace?!?!! *(You're hired again. More of this please. Ed.)*

HERE they are — Glenda's Cheese-cake Chippendales (geddit?)!
JOHN LATSIS — He's the munchy Stavros with Loadsamoney whose just shelled out millions to the Tories?!! How'd ya like to put a deposit in *my* account, Big Boy??!?
ANTON MOSSIMAN — I'm one little dish that could do with some attention!?! Over here with your giant pepperpot, Anton!?! (Geddit?!)
SIR ROLAND SMITH — Boring name, boring guy!!

Byeeeee!

"Things might have been worse, Marie — we might have been torn to pieces by the tabloids"

Prosecution – The Oldest Profession

by Dr Anthony Clarevoyeur

SINCE time immemorial men have felt the need for prosecution and have sought out prosecutes to find relief for their inner tensions.

Sir Allan Green is only one in a long tradition of lawyers who like to dress up and engage in bizarre rituals in order to put people into prison.

Why is it that perfectly ordinary men who could obtain satisfaction in any number of professions seek excitement by hanging around the dimly lit corridors of the seedy Law Courts in the run-down Old Bailey area, waiting to "pick up" their clients?

There can be no doubt that these figures, many of them well-educated family men, risk everything by engaging in dangerous legal activities.

Why do they do it? Perhaps we shall never know. But it is possible that such men do these things because they have an unconscious urge to be in court *(shurely 'be caught'? Ed).*

(That's enough. Ed.)

Alternative Rocky Horror Service Book

No. 94: A Service of Condonation For The Victims Of Social Deprivation In Inner-City Areas

The Archbishop of Canterbury *(for it is he):* Dearly beloved yobboes, we are gathered together here today to give thanks for the spontaneous expression of anger and frustration which took place last night on the N— or M— Estate *(here he may name Mandela or Poulson, or whomsoever shall be appropriate).*

We give heartfelt and humble thanks to the media for the wonderful coverage they have given to these celebratory observances.

All: Get on with it, mate.

(Here shall be shown an video of the burning of Mr V.J. Patel's Grocery and Newsagent's shop by members of the congregation)

All: Look, there's Dave — kick his head in, Dave *(or they may make similar responses).*

The President: Let us pray.

All: Piss off, baldy, and show us the video of Jason doin' a handbrake turn in Mr Ramshad's Nissan Cherry.

(A second video may here be screened, showing a ramraider entering the premises of the Bank of Bangladesh, T. Dan Smith Road. All shall then spontaneously sing TIDINGS OF COMFORT AND JOYRIDING)

Archbishop: O Government, who art in 10 Downing Street, *Hello* be thy magazine. We pray to thee most earnestly that thou wilst look mercifully upon those who live and don't work in our inner cities. As everyone knowest except thou, this state of deprivation has risen through underfunding and lack of resources, and can only be remedied by massive injections of sorely needed investment to revitalise the infrastructure. Grant that thy servant Heseltine may be inspired to move us to the top of his agenda.

All: What's he on about? What a poof! Someone nick his hat — it's covered in gold.

The Laying-On Of Hands

(Here the congregation shall gather round the celebrant and lay hands upon him, taking unto themselves whatsoever they may deem to be of value. They may then set fire to the church)

All: 'Ere we go, 'ere we go, 'ere we go...

The 10 rules the ITC followed in picking the new franchises

1. The quality of programmes offered in the prospectus will be the deciding factor in all cases unless it isn't.

2. The highest bidder will automatically be offered the franchise, except in most cases.

3. Bidders offering no money and no quality will be unlikely to granted a franchise, except in the case of Central TV.

4. In the case of any company offering a ridiculously large sum to the Treasury in the hope of ensuring that they retain their franchise, we will give them a nasty shock. N.B. TVS.

5. Any consortium including Mr Melvyn Bragg shall automatically be accepted, in recognition of his outstanding contributions to contemporary culture.

6. Any of the many consortia including David Frost shall not be deemed acceptable. This clause is never to be revealed to anybody.

7. Granada TV, the flagship of quality commercial television, maker of *Coronation Street*, is to be kept in at the personal request of the Prime Minister, although he could do without *World In Action*.

8. Thames TV is to be axed, as a last gesture of respect to the late Supreme Ruler of the Universe, M. Thatch, whose many achievements include dreaming up these ridiculous rules.

9. Er...

10. That's it.

NEW MEDAL FOR SIR ALLAN

It's the King's Cross

THAT US SENATE SEX HEARING IN FULL

Day 94

SENATOR HIRAM J. COCKLEBURGER *(presiding):* We must now continue with the hearing of testimony as to why Judge John Thomas should or should not be admitted as a judge of the Very Supreme Court of these United States of the USA.

OTHER SENATORS: Get on with it, let's get to where they talk dirty.

SENATOR EDWARD KOPECHNE *(shurely 'Chappaquiddick? Ed):* Ah can put mah hand on mah heart, mah fellow Americans, and say that nevah in all mah life have I been so shocked as by the truly vicious and shocking rumours that I have been spreading around in recent weeks about the way this man has behaved towards a poor defenceless woman, suffering harassment in her place of work. The place for that kind of thing in a modern society is in a beach bungalow in the Kennedy compound at Palm Beach.

SENATOR JOSEPH KINNOCK: Never once since the dawn of time has such a totally, utterly and totally utterly immoral act been perpetrated, committed and totally perpetrated by a man on a woman.

SENATOR COCKLE-BURGER: May I remind this Committee that we have not yet heard any evidence upon which to base a judgement on this matter. Call Professor Fanny Hill, the Professor of Feminist Legal Studies at the University of New Dworkin.

PROFESSOR HILL *(pointing at black man in suit):* That's the one, it was him who done it.

COCKLEBURGER: Professor, could I prevail upon you to describe in your own explicit words and in some graphic detail, bearing in mind that this hearing is now on prime time television and being conveyed by satellite to the whole of mankind, just what he did, when and how?

PROFESSOR HILL: Indeedy-doody, sir, so I

will. It is my duty, under God, so to do. Are you all listening carefully?

(Heavy breathing from Senator Kennedy)

HILL: On one occasion, Judge John Thomas approached my work station one morning and made a number of explicit personal remarks, including the words "Good morning, Fanny", "Have a nice day" and "My penis is twelve yards long".

(Gasps of shock and pleasure from ageing senators)

FLOOR MANAGER: Can you say that again, sweetheart? More emphasis on the word "penis", and then we'll go into the big sequence on the porno videos, OK? You're doing great. Relax, have fun, let's go.

PROF HILL: I would also like to recall the occasion when I was sitting there in my own body space when the accused invaded my contact zone by offering me a cup of coffee with the words: "Is this hot enough for you?" There was no mistaking the intimidatory verbal

rape that was perpetrated in this statement.

SENATOR KOPECHNE: And when this outrage had been perpetrated, what was your reaction? Did you feel violated, disgusted, dirty? Did you feel as if you were drowning in an automobile that had driven off a bridge? *(Shurely 'sea of filth'? Ed.)*

HILL: My immediate reaction was to forget all about it for ten years until I heard on TV that Judge Thomas was the conservative nominee for the Supreme Court.

SENATOR LEGOVER: Back in the great state of South Semolina, where ah come from, folks are mighty worried about this very grave and important issue of sexual harassmentation in the workplace and in the place of work. We believe firmly in the essential dignity of women of every creed and gender, which is why, as a Senator of the United States, I believe it is my firm and resolute duty to suck up *(shurely 'stand up'? Ed)* to this very important lobby.

COCKLEBURGER: Bring on the little black fellow with the glasses.

TREVOR MACDONALD *(for it is he):* Bong! The Senate confirms Judge in Harassment Case. Dong! It's a close thing, but Bush gets his man in. Bonk! And those Samoans beat Wales by 133 to nil.

COCKLEBURGER: Could we now have the newly confirmed appointee?

JUDGE THOMAS *(for it is he at last):* Ah just want to say that never before in the history of human conflict has any man suffered, as I have, such mendacity, ignominy, traducity, smearment, falsification, slanderation and endragment through the mire of malicious innuendizement. Ah can truly say that I would rather be lynched on a tree by the Ku Klux Klan than to endure the ordeal of such traducement, smearity, mendation, fellatio...

COCKLEBURGER: Thank you, judge, we all enjoyed that very much. But we're just coming up to a commercial break, so there's just time for a quick prayer from our well-loved Senate Chaplain, the Rev J.C. Flannelbacker.

FLANNELBACKER: Praise the Lord. Let he who is without sin cast the first vote against our brother. For verily, I say to you, America may never be the same again should this stain be allowed to remain upon our flag. *(Sings)* "Oh say, can't you see, By the dawn's early light..."

(Weeping senators all join in. Screen fills with commercial for Old Uncle Sam's All-American Apple Pie)

VOICE OVER: Pure, wholesome, clean and lifegiving. That's what the American Way is all about.

DIRECTOR: OK, cut studio. That was great, everyone.

(Hearing room empties as senators adjourn for urgent appointments with call-girls, coke dealers, Mafia hitmen etc)

MAKERS OF THE TWENTIETH CENTURY

The Sunday Times Guide to the 1000 Most Important People of the 20th Century

Week 94: Mussolini to Miller

BENITO MUSSOLINI
Italian dictator who was hanged upside-down with his mistress.

MADONNA
b. Anne-Maria Tagliatelli in 1958
Singer, composer and cultural icon. Her genius first expressed itself in the seminal 1983 album *Give Me Your Love Heat Now, Big Boy* and continued throughout the 80s and 90s as a dominant influence on the artistic and intellectual life of the modern world. Her innovative dress style centred on metal underwear and became a post-feminist totem for a whole generation.

YEHUDI MENUHIN
Violinist. Best known as teacher of Nigel Kennedy *(q.v.)*

HAROLD MACMILLAN
Politician whose career was destroyed by sexy call girl Christine Keeler *(q.v.)*

MONTY PYTHON
Seminal TV comedian of the 60s who pioneered surrealism in the visual arts. Inspired numerous imitators, including the Goons, Hancock and *Beyond The Fringe*. Sketches included "Dead Gerbil", *The Steeplejack Song* and "Huge Foot Crushing Little Man In Desert".

NELSON MANDELA
Great African statesman. Husband of Winnie *(see below)*.

MILLICENT MARTIN
Leading satirist of the 60s whose irreverent

songs brought down the Macmillan government *(see above)*.

VYACHESLAV MOLOTOV
Inventor of the cocktail.

MAO TSE-TUNG
Chinese leader, now discredited.

KYLIE MINOGUE
Outstanding actress of the 80s, star of universally acclaimed drama series *Neighbours*. Also became well-known singer, famous for experimental hit albums *Kylie Sings Waltzing Matilda And Other Well-Loved Australian Songs*, *Kylie Has A Party* and *Kylie Has A Party II*.

MAGGIE
Nickname of Margaret Thatcher *(see pp 106-134 under Greatest Women of Century)*.

RUPERT MURDOCH
Global communicator, philanthropist and Christian evangelist. Born 1931 at Billabong Creek, NSW. Educated Eton, Winchester and Oxford University, where he won First-Class Honours in all subjects. After a short spell as brain surgeon and astronaut, he was appointed editor of Australia's leading agricultural journal, *Sheep and Sheepshaggers*, which happened to be owned by his father. Within a year he had invented the famous picture of a naked sheep on page three, which made the journal the highest-selling paper in the Australian sheep trade. As a result of this trail-blazing triumph, his father gave him enough money to buy the ailing London newspaper *The Times*. Within days Murdoch had changed the title to the *Sun* and, by transforming its old-fashioned format and contents, achieved sales of 7 billion copies a day, a world record. By a brilliant series of business coups, he then managed to buy up every newspaper, television station and film studio in America. But perhaps his greatest achievement was the invention of the satellite dish, which enabled him to lose millions of pounds every day. *(You're fired. R.M.)*

ROBERT MAXWELL
Fat idiot. *(You're reinstated. R.M.)*

DR JONATHAN MILLER
Uomo universale, wit, polymath, neurosurgeon, director, sage, onion. *(That's enough Makers of the Twentieth Century. Ed.)*

"Do exactly as we say, Mr Briggs, or the Snowman gets it"

Deirdre Spart's 10 tell-tale ways to prove that you're being sexually harassed (and should take your case to the European Court of Human Rights)

1. Your boss is a man.

2. He looks at you in a funny way, especially when you come in late.

3. He goes out of his way to say "Good morning" when you enter the office.

4. He comments on your dress in a suggestive way, e.g. "Can you please hang up your coat, I keep on tripping over it."

5. He tries to engage you in improper conversation, e.g. "Did you see *Inspector Morse* on TV last night?"

6. He makes overt gestures in your presence, such as scratching parts of his body, e.g. his head.

7. Er...

8, 9, 10. That's it.

HUNT UNDER CRITICISM

by Our Countryside Staff **Jeremy Beagle, James Hunt, Samantha Fox** and **Mark Tully-Ho**

ONE OF the most famous and prestigious hunts, The Porn, is under fire from the League Against Cruel Sports following a series of incidents earlier this year.

The Porn, which numbers such distinguished figures as Lord Rothermere, Lord Stevens and Captain Maxwell MC, has traditionally hunted members of the Royal Family, using packs of newshounds. This has long been regarded in England as a time-honoured sport and part of the rich pageant that is English life.

Gone to Front Cover

However, a number of recent incidents, some of them captured on video, have brought the hunt into disrepute. In one disgusting incident, a group of hounds pursued their quarry, Princess Diana, to a remote Mediterranean beach where they proceeded to take photos of her in a bikini.

On another occasion, they captured Prince Andrew totally naked and defenceless and snapped at him mercilessly.

Worst of all was the helpless figure of Prince Harry tossed to the newshounds as he relieved himself behind a bush.

The huge outcry against such cruelty has provoked a demand for a new code of hunting to prevent this sort of thing happening again.

Said one senior Huntsman: "I am deeply distressed that these stories appeared in someone else's paper. Let's see those pics again."

STOP PRESS

No one to resign over Porn shocker.

The Alternative Rocky Horror Service Book

No. 94: A Service For The Evangelisation Of The Islamic Community (© *Carey and Sharey Publications, Lambeth, 1991*)

The President: Praise be to Allah.

All: Yes indeed. Allah is the greatest.

The President: There is only one God and Mohammed is his prophet.

All: Death to Rushdie.

There shall then be a reading from the Holy Koran, or from some other suitable text.

President: The infidels must be slain.

All: It is the only language that they understand.

The Homily

(to be delivered by the Archbishop of Canterbury)

Dearly beloved, we are instructed by the Lord to go out into the world and bear witness to the good news of our Lord Jesus Christ, who as all Muslims accept was quite an important prophet in his own way. This surely must bind us together with all our Islamic brethren and lead us to live in harmony without trying to force our beliefs down other people's throats or expecting them to live according to the norms of our own ethnic group.

All: Amen to that. Can we burn the books now?

The Congregation shall then gather round the alter and show their non-judgemental, even-handedness by burning copies of The Satanic Verses *and the* New Testament. *All shall now sing from the* Cat Stevens Hymns for Today.

"Allah things bright and beautiful...
Allah things great and small."

THE BOOK OF ~~JOB~~ BOB

Chapter One

1. And, lo, there dwelt in the land of Pergam-on a man, mighty in girth, whose name was Bob. And the Lord blest Bob, and showered him with earthly blessings.

2. For he gaveth unto his servant Bob many sons and daughters and riches greater than any man could reckon.

3. And Bob praised the Lord mightily, for he said: "Surely I am the most fortunate of men. For do I not have many mansions, a yacht forty cubits long and many servants?

4. "And am I not known unto all the mighty ones of the world, a friend to princes and potentates, yea even unto Cea-ces-cu?

5. But the Lord looketh upon his servant Bob and saith unto himself: "Here is a man who hath become puffed up like unto the bull-frog that sitteth upon the lily-pad that is in the pools of Sha-ron and Tra-cey."

6. And, from that time, the Lord turneth away his face from Bob. And he sent unto him a succession of plagues to try him, each worse than the one which went before.

7. And the first of these plagues was the plague of debts. For Bob had bitten off more than he could cheweth.

8. And the moneylenders waxed wroth with Bob, and demanded of him that he should return unto them all that he had taken from them on usury, even an billion-fold or twain.

9. And this putteth the wind up Bob, even as the wind that bloweth the tear gas across the lands of Gaza. For Bob looketh into his treasury and findeth it empty.

10. Then came a second plague, even more terrible than the first. For this was the plague of hacks, who rose up against him, crying mightily, saying: "Bob, thou has been thoroughly investigated and we can exclusively reveal that thou art not only bankrupt and an frightful crook, but that thou hast also for many years been privily an agent of the following organisations — viz. Mossad, the KGB, the Securitate, you name it, thou hast been in it up to thy neck."

11. And, lo, there was among the hacks a man called Hersh, who said unto Bob: "I charge thee that it was thou who betrayed Van-u-nu into the hands of Shamir, that he might be cast even into the deepest dungeon that is in the land of Is-rael."

12. Then Bob was sore cast down. For he kneweth that his number was up.

13. And he saw coming over the horizon a cloud of troubles that would engulf him, even as the world was engulfed by the Great Flood in the time of Noah.

14. And so Bob called unto him his captains and his servants and he saith: "Make ready my ship, that is forty cubits long and twenty cubits high. For I will go forth upon the waters of the deep and speak to the Lord about all these troubles which have come upon my head."

15. And it was about the fifth hour of the day, when the earth was still in darkness, that they came unto the land of Can-ary.

16. And whilst the servants of Bob were asleep, Bob casteth off his raiment, strode upon the deck, and crieth out with an loud voice: "Lord, Lord, deliver me from mine troubles."

17. Then the Lord sent a great fish, which is called Leviathan. And the fish swimmeth through the waters and swalloweth up Bob with an mighty gulp.

18. And after three days the fish vomiteth forth Bob, even upon the Mount of Olives.

19. And all the sons of Israel gathered in that place to see this wondrous thing that had come to pass.

20. And they said one unto the other: "All praise to the servant of the Lord, Bob, who was surely the greatest man that ever walked upon the earth."

Here endeth the Book of Bob.

"We sort of had our hearts set on something round"

Agatha Christie's
MURDER ON THE LADY GHISLAINE

I N HIS lavish office on the 24th floor of the headquarters of the Mutual Provident Life Association, Sir Hector Prune was looking at a file marked MAXWELL with a furrowed brow.

"This could mean the biggest accident claim in our company's history," he said to his assistant, Mr Archibald Wetherington. "There is £20 million at stake here, unless we can prove that it was suicide."

"But he was murdered, Sir. Everyone knows that. It even says so in the *Daily Telegraph*," Wetherington replied.

Both men stared at each other gloomily. Then the Chairman's assistant had a flash of inspiration. "I say, sir," he cried, "I've just had an idea. I sometimes go shooting with a chap called Hastings. Pretty dim sort of fellow."

"Oh yes," replied Sir Hector, "he's the editor of the *Telegraph*, isn't he?"

"No, sir, another chap called Hastings. He works for that very famous Belgian detective, Hercule Poirot. You've probably seen him on television."

"Yes, Wetherington, so what are you suggesting?"

"Well, sir, I thought I might give him a ring…"

—☆—

T HE well-groomed figure of Poirot sat sipping a glass of anise outside the famous Cafe de Noel Coward on the colourful quayside of the old port in Tenerife.

"Jolly hot," said his companion, Captain Hastings, loosening his heavy tweed overcoat a couple of buttons.

Poirot did not reply. He was already deep in thought. Finally he fixed his friend with a quizzical smile.

"Most curious, Hastings, eez it not, zat ze last known words of Monsieur Maxwell were to give ze order for ze air-conditioning to be turned down? And yet, as you can see, eet eez very hot 'ere."

To emphasise the point he took a large scarlet handkerchief from his top pocket and brushed the drops of perspiration from his immaculately waxed moustache.

"Furzer, 'astings, ze great tycoon ate 'is last meal in zis very restaurant, at ze very next table to where we are sitting. And look, it is set for *two* persons. Curious, eez it not, mon brave?"

As usual Hastings was finding it rather difficult to follow the great man's train of thought.

"Surely, Poirot, the whole thing's pretty damned obvious. Chap's business affairs getting into a spot of bother. Lot of chaps saying he's a bit dodgy. Takes a holiday to get away from it all. Gets depressed. Chucks himself overboard."

"We shall see, 'astings, we shall see," was Poirot's enigmatic reply.

—☆—

I NSPECTOR Knackeros of the Guardia di Tenerife guided the little launch with deft skill alongside the sparkling white bulwarks of the luxurious yacht, the Lady Ghislaine.

Poirot shivered slightly as they clambered up onto the deck of the doom-laden vessel.

"You could have saved yourself the trouble, Señor," said the inspector, flashing a smile with his stained teeth.

"It was natural causes. An open and shut case. You see, here is where the Englishman fell over the side. It was his favourite spot. He would often sit here in the early morning, with no clothes on, reading a copy of his life story by Joseph Haines. They are eccentric, the Ingleesh, no?"

While the policeman explained his theory as to how the mystery which had baffled the world had come about, Poirot was on his hands and knees minutely examining the well-scrubbed deck.

A careful observer might have noted Poirot placing a huge half-finished pot of caviar labelled FINEST BELUGA — FOR KGB USE ONLY into his handkerchief.

"You won't find anything there, sir," broke in the commanding tones of Captain Goodfellow RN. "My lads have been over the whole ship from top sail to bilges with a fine-tooth comb."

"They haven't found anything at all," insisted a tanned Scandinavian girl in a bikini who had just come up the companion-way from the Master Cabin.

Hastings cast an appreciative eye over her shapely form, undoing another button of his overcoat.

"Ah," said the Captain, "let me introduce you gentlemen to Miss Ingrid Smorgesbord. She was helping Mr Maxwell with some important... er... research."

But Poirot's attention had already been drawn to a black balaclava secreted behind a lifebelt on the bulkhead above him.

"What do you make of zees, 'astings?" said the great detective. "A woolly 'at wiz ze letters M-O-S-S clearly visible."

"Perhaps it was hired from Moss Bros, Poirot," Hastings offered.

"Per'aps, 'astings. We shall see," Poirot replied. "I sink eet eez time to exercise ze little grey cells n'est-ce pas?"

—☆—

 ATER, in the luxury stateroom, Poirot was questioning the twenty-four members of the crew. As he cast his expert eye round their faces, he felt a twinge of familiarity.

Didn't that deckhand there, in his matelot's cap and plainly false moustache, bear an uncanny resemblance to the former Ambassador to Washington, Sir Peter Jaybotham?

And the shifty-looking stoker in the corner? He could easily be mistaken for Joe Haines, the celebrated political commentator.

And what about the fair-haired barman with glasses? Didn't he look remarkably like Nick Davies, the discredited former *Mirror* Foreign Editor and international arms dealer?

The Captain broke into Poirot's reflections with a dismissive laugh. "You're wasting your time, Poirot, if you think any of us did it. We all loved him like a father, didn't we boys?"

The members of the crew immediately took out onions from their pockets and began to weep inconsolably.

Poirot's eyes narrowed. This was becoming a most interesting case.

Hastings, deeply moved, undid another button of his tweed overcoat.

(*To be continued*)

MAXWELL

Tributes pour in as world mourns

President Nicolae Ceausescu

"He was a true friend of mankind, a great leader and a world statesman."

President Leonid Brezhnev

"Hullo Bob, or is it dosvidenyah! All we worked for together has come to nothing. But that's life!"

President Todor Zhivkov

"The world today seems a much smaller place without Comrade Bob, the bravest, most loyal friend the Bulgarian people ever had."

Marshal Josef Stalin

"I salute the memory of Comrade Maxwell, the most gallant soldier of World War Two. I look forward to welcoming him down here for many millions of hours of happy talk about the old days."

President Ernst Honecker

"As we say in my country: Sieg Heil, Bob. Du bist ein gute freund von der Deutsche Demokratische Republik. Sorry about the 10 million marks I owe you, but now the Czech is in the past. Geddit? Ha ha ha!"

Prime Minister John Major

"In my judgement Robert Maxwell was a larger-than-life character who made a very considerable contribution to this country's life in a number of different ways. Oh yes."

(That's enough tributes to Maxwell. Ed.)

BOAT PEOPLE TO BE REPATRIATED

by Our Nonsense Staff **E. Lear**

PROTESTS mounted today as a large number of so-called Jumblies were ordered to return home after their illegal immigration to the Lands of the Western Sea.

Having survived a perilous journey in a craft which was little more than a sieve, the Jumblies were said to be furious at their enforced repatriation to the Far and Few Lands where they originally lived.

"This is racism," said one spokesman. "Just because our heads are green and our hands are blue, no one wants to know."

An official denied this, and said that the Jumblies were not genuine refugees and that the Sieve-People were in fact economic migrants.

"They have already bought an owl, a useful cart, a pound of rice and a cranberry tart," he said. "Not to mention bees, a pig, some green jackdaws and a lovely monkey with lollipop paws."

The Jumblies return to an uncertain future at home, convinced that no one "cares a button or gives a fig".

Edward Lear is 107.

Guilty prisoner discovered shock

by Our Legal Correspondents **Joshua Rosencrantz** and **Joshua Guiltyswine**

THE LEGAL world was rocked to its foundations yesterday when the Court of Appeal found that a man convicted of murder on seventeen counts was, in fact, guilty of the crimes he claimed to have committed.

Extensive forensic tests have shown that police evidence produced at this trial in 1986 was in fact authentic.

"This makes a mockery of traditional judicial procedure in this country," said Inspector Knacker. "I suppose there's always one good apple in the barrel," the controversial inspector went on, "but we will soon find him and sort him out."

Lord Denning is 209.

The World's Worst Columnist

PETER McLIE

HAVE you noticed that there's very little in the newspapers at the moment? Leafing through them, I can find nothing to write about.

Isn't this indicative of the sorry state of journalism today?

☐ **SHOES are something I notice everyone is wearing.**

Could this be because Fergie is a confirmed shoe-wearer?

How pathetic that we should all ape the Royal Family by donning these ridiculous articles of footwear.

Take them off, Ma'am, and maybe we'll follow your example.

☐ *I READ in the previous paragraph a man writing about shoes.*

What a sad reflection on modern journalism that these overpaid scribblers can think of nothing better to write about.

I SEE the moaning minnies are up in arms at some poor columnist who had the audacity to write about shoes in a London newspaper.

Whatever next? Surely the honest scribe can make an item of interest out of anything, however trivial.

☐ *HAVE you noticed how editors are quite happy to print any old rubbish in their pages these days?*

I notice in the London Evening Standard, for instance, a man writing a whole item about shoes.

Where will it end? A man writing about a man writing about shoes?

It all adds up to a pretty sad commentary on the state of journalism today.

"He's doing a ten-year stretch for fraud — only been inside two days!"

DAILY Mirror

Friday, December 20, 1991   **LAST WITH THE NEWS**   25p

WORLD EXCLUSIVE

MAXWELL VERY FAT

by Our Investigative Staff
RICHARD STOAT, CHARLES
WEASEL, MARJE DUPES and
JOE SHAMES.

AFTER months of painstaking, no-holds-barred investigation, Mirror newsmen have pieced together the amazing truth behind Robert Maxwell.

- ● HE WAS INCREDIBLY FAT

- ● HE PAID US ALL A LOT OF MONEY

- ● HE IS DEAD

- ● THIS MEANS WE CAN ALL NOW SAY HOW FAT HE WAS

These horrifying revelations must change forever the world's view of the man the world knew as Captain Bob.

We admit it — we were duped.

Like millions of others, we thought Maxwell was very thin.

After all, he told us so himself. Often he would ring us up in the middle of the night and say "I'm thin, aren't I?"

And we'd all say, "Gosh, sir, yes you are — you're the thinnest man on earth."

But now that the full terrifying truth has come to light, thanks to the fearless investiga-

tion by the brave Mirror team, we now know that we were hoodwinked.

The Mirror is not ashamed to admit it made an honest mistake.

Who knows what astonishing new facts about Maxwell we will publish tomorrow?

Order your copy of the Sun today.

THE FAT FILE

by Top Investigative Mirrorman PAUL FAT

These are the shocking statistics which prove beyond a shadow of doubt that the late Robert Maxwell was one of the fattest men in the history of the world.

Waist: 217 kilometres

Inside Leg: 2 Hectares

Chest: Empty

Neck: 3,412 ecu

In an average year, Maxwell consumed 28,416 tonnes of food.

We have obtained a top-secret copy of the menu for

the mid-morning "snack" consumed by Mr Maxwell on 24 June 1990.

INSIDE – ALL YOUR FAVOURITE MIRROR FEATURES

The Sad Case of the Defrauded Pensioner

A MRS LUDMILLA Tolpuddle, 78, a former employee of a very well known Fleet Street newspaper, has written to me with a tragic story.

When she went in to collect her pension cheque last month, she was told that there was no more money.

When she asked "Why?" she was told that all the money in the newspaper's pension fund had been stolen by a fat, bloated, caviar-guzzling capitalist swine.

Apparently he had bought the newspaper precisely in order to defraud honest working men and women like Mrs Tolpuddle.

There is no doubt who was to blame for this appalling scandal:

● **Mrs Thatcher and the Tory government.**

By failing to introduce proper legal safeguards on the multi-million-pound pension funds they have created not just one new "Tolpuddle martyr" but a whole generation of them.

YET ANOTHER MISCARRIAGE OF JUSTICE

● **A Mr Kevin M. and his brother Ian have written to me from Ford Open Prison saying that they are totally innocent of the crimes of which they have been accused,.**

After an initial inspection of the files, it is clear to me that "The Maxwell Two" are totally innocent. Why is the Establishment hounding these men, so soon after they have lost their father in a tragic accident?

It is now clear that the only person responsible for the so-called theft of £526 million from the Mirror pension fund was Thatcher.

I appeal to Kenneth Baker to string this woman up now. It is the only language these people understand.

THE THINGS THEY SAY

❝ I always knew he was a crook — but he provided me with a valuable cheque ❞ *(surely 'platform for addressing the working-class audience'? Ed) — Pol Fot*

If you would like me to investigate Robert Maxwell, you must be joking. Don't ring me, Paul Foot, on 0898 74387624.

Jerusalem – European to be buried on Mount of Olives

FOR the first time in history a newspaper is to receive Israel's highest honour by being buried at the country's most sacred spot, the Mount of Olives. An enormous hole, 586 cubits deep, in accordance with Talmudic law, is to be dug in the side of the mountain to accommodate millions of unsold copies of *The European*. Israel's President Mr Chaim Herzog said: "*The European* was a newspaper of almost mythical boredom. It will be sorely missed by no one at all."

Spot the players and win your own football club!

MIRROR SPORT

RULES OF COMPETITION

LOOK carefully at this picture of a recent match between Oxford United and Derby County. See if you can identify the whereabouts of the players. *(Clue: They have all been sold.)*

ANDY CAPP

My naughty nights with 'The Captain'

Joella tells all

"He seduced me and then left me feeling dirty."

That was how a tearful Joella Haynes, 64, described her steamy nights of shame with the world's fattest man.

"To start with, he was charming. During those first weeks he made me feel like a million dollars, which is what he paid me.

"All I had to do, as he put it, was to 'lie with him'.

"He showered me with gifts — I had a desk of my own, a typewriter, a chair, and a lavish supply of paper.

"It was then that he asked me to perform a number of disgusting and unnatural acts in order to gratify him."

Domination

"He expected me to write an obscene book, full of outrageous fantasies, called *Maxwell — Portrait Of A Genius.*

"And still he wasn't satisfied. When we had finished, he wanted more. He wanted *Portrait Of A Genius Vol. 2.*

"He wanted a column at least once a week — it was exhausting.

"Wherever I was in the world, he would ring up in the middle of the night, telling me to 'put it in' or 'take it out'. It was disgusting. I began to feel used."

Crossing her legs provocatively in her 18th-floor office at the *Daily Mirror* building, Joella said defiantly: "I won't do just anything for money. I'm not a prostitute, you know.

"This whole business has been the most terrible shock to me," she concluded. "After all, it is not every day you discover what a terrible creep you are."

WIN WITH THE MIRROR!

This 68-year-old pensioner from Oxford won a staggering

£526 million

from the Mirror, just by filling in a form.

Mr R.M. asked for no publicity for his world record win. He told the Mirror: "I would like this kept quiet." But he admitted that he was planning a cruise to the Canary Islands.

He added: "The £526 million will not make any difference to my life, because I owe four times that amount already."

CHILDREN IN NEED

Spare a thought this Christmas for little Kevin and Ian. This time last year they were looking forward to Christmas turkey and vintage champagne. Now they have only the prospect of porridge.

All they will get in their stockings is a letter from the Serious Fraud Office. They are bankrupt, disgraced and have been cruelly treated by their father.

If you have any spare money at this time, for heaven's sake hang on to it.

Issued by Children in Need

(Patron HRH The Esther of Ranthzen)

PETER McLIE

The World's Worst Columnist

I OBSERVE many shop windows are displaying an old man with a white beard and a long red coat. Who can this be I wonder? He seems perfectly harmless by the look of him but I am not so sure. Perhaps one day we will be given an explanation by the powers that be. And none to soon.

☐ J.P. HARTLEY *does not exist, I have discovered. Yet his book is a best-seller. What a con.*

☐ I WAS in a restaurant recently, and the waiter brought me a very clever new device for eating soup.

It has a small concave receptacle at one end, attached to a long handle at the other.

You pick up the soup and lift it to your mouth while it's still hot.

In my day in Peterhead we had to drink our broth straight from the bowl — and a right mess we made of it!

Let us hope some clever fellow like Sir Clive Sinclair can find a way to manufacture this brilliant British invention.

He could make millions — even in this recession.

☐ *I SPENT a weekend at the seaside recently and noticed a curious thing. Sometimes the sea was near the shore and sometimes it was quite a distance away. Why was this, I wonder? Is it anything to do with global warming? If so, it is a frightening thought that the sea can be affected like this. But just suppose the leaves in the streets are in some way connected with it. Then would it be a surprise to discover that the old bearded man in red is behind the whole thing? (You're fired. Ed.)*

"I'm sorry, sir, the Alabama train gets very full — you'll have to put that on your knee"

Winter Olympics results

Cross-Country Skating — Men's 4x400 miles

Gold: Findus Fishfingers *(Finland)*
Silver: Conrad Moosejaw *(Canada)*
Bronze: Dolmio Tomato *(Italy)*

Synchronised Ice-Jumping (Men's)

Gold: Bjorn Free *(Sweden)*
Silver: Bjorn Yesterday *(Denmark)*
Bronze: Juan Bjorn Everiminute *(Spain)*

Indoor Freestyle Bobsleigh Dancing (Men's)

Gold: Yurin Samplov *(former Soviet Union)*
Silver: Ingrid Steroid *(formerly an East German woman)*
Bronze: Eddie "The Eagle" Edwards *(formerly famous)*

Women's Downhill Volleyball

Gold: Karen Daterape *(USA)*
Silver: Omega Stopwatch *(Czechoslovakia)*
Bronze: Vanilla Haagen-Dazs *(Holland)*

Mixed Speed Snowman Building (new event)

Gold: Frei and Lørie *(Norway)*
Silver: Toksvig and McShane *(Canada)*
Bronze: Anderson and Andandersonson *(Iceland)*

(That's enough Winter Olympics. Ed.)

Come on, this must be worth a few points, surely...

'I WAS MAD' says David Oik

by Our Religious Staff
Sir Clifford Richard

THE former leader of the minority political party, the Social Democrats, Mr David Oik last night admitted frankly that he had "been mad" when he claimed to be the saviour of Britain.

"It was all the fault of the media," said the colourful Doctor Oik who had shocked the nation with his bizarre claims about proportional representation and breaking the mould.

"I was under a great deal of stress and I suppose I just flipped."

"I now realise that I was not the Messiah at all. It was a silly thing to say. My real name as everybody knows is Dr Napoleon Bonaparte and I come from the planet Venus with greetings from the great Zog of Moab."

Dr David Owen is 46.

Is history dead?

*Asks **Norman Stone**, Professor of Modern History at the University of Oxford*

In his fascinating new book, Mr Fushida Fujiyama asks: "Is history dead?" My answer is simple. I hope it is, because then I won't have to do any more work and I can spend all my time in the pub.

© *The Sunday Times*

NEXT WEEK:
AM I DEAD? by Paul Johnson

A Doctor writes

As a doctor, I am often asked: "Doctor, will you come and see me, please. I know it's past midnight, but my wife is very ill."

Well, the simple answer is:

"This is a recorded message. The surgery times are between 9.30 and 11.00 on alternate Tuesdays. Thank you for calling."

© A. Doctor.

CRICKET THE BOTHAM WAY

1 Cricket is all about timing. So don't time the World Cup to coincide with the vital panto at the Basildon Hexagon.

2 Cricket is a team game. So don't worry if you have an off day. Off playing Widow Twankey at the Leeds Apollo. You can rely on your team mates to do the hard work.

THE PART OF IAN BOTHAM WILL BE PLAYED BY DEREK PRINGLE

3 Practice is absolutely vital. Panto is a very demanding game. So don't waste any time in the nets when you could be preparing your "Hello Boys and Girls" routine.

Five minutes, Mr Botham

Yeah, that's enough rehearsal

4 Keep your Eye on the Ball. The Ball scene is the toughest part of *Cinderella*, and if you don't pay 100 per cent attention you could be caught out by TV's Christopher Biggins as the Ugly Sister.

5 Pace yourself. Don't waste your most laughable performance on the cricket field. Save it for the first interval closer with Panto's Bob Carolgees and Spit the Dog.

HA HA HA HA HA

WRONG

6 Don't argue with the umpire. Save it for the audience.

You're useless!

Oh no I'm not!

Oh yes you are!

The Daily Hellograph

FINAL

ESTABLISHED 1855   NO. 42,339

40p

LONDON AND MANCHESTER

FRIDAY, JANUARY 31, 1992

Desert Island Disco!

Heartwarming *Hellograph* pictures as fifty years of celebrity castaways toast radio's most heartwarming show

**Photographs by "Call" Nikon Ross   Captions by Jane Thynne-Stuff
Idea by Max Hastings**

Top DJ Alan "Fluff" Freeman chats to Sir Robin Butler, Secretary to the Cabinet. Sir Robin asked for one of Mrs Thatcher's speeches as record number seven. Alan's luxury was herbal tea.

Broadcaster Benny Green with Gayle Hunnicut. Benny's book was *Not out! The Life of Don Bradman*, written by himself.

Top football star Ray Clemence teams up with famous Fatwah victim Salman Rushdie. As a special concession, Salman's episode was recorded in a safe house. He asked if he could take the Koran instead of the Bible. And Sue said yes.

Sir Peter Hall and Marlene Dietrich (castaway no. 13,704,152). "I've been on three times," says Marlene. "And every time I chose a bath of asses' milk as my luxury." Sir Peter Hall startled Roy Plomley by choosing eight Stockhausen records.

One-time student revolutionary Tariq Ali arrives with Rula Lenska (castaway no. 1794). Tariq created a stir when he chose The Red Flag as record number three.

Lord Forte shares a culinary castaway joke with TV chef Fanny Craddock. She annoyed Michael Parkinson by choosing a MagiMix food processor as a luxury. "Don't be daft," he said in a celebrated exchange. "There's no fookin' electricity on t'island." Shortly afterwards Michael left the show.

The late Reginald Bosanquet was the surprise guest, seen here arriving with Lady Olga Maitland. Asked if he would try to escape, Reggie replied: "Is there any booze in this studio?" The programme was never transmitted.

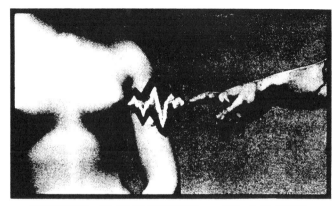

THE SOUTH ⚡ BANK ⚡ MANAGER SHOW

Introduced by MELVYN BARG

(Jazzed-up Paganini played by Julian Lloyds-Bank)

BARG: Tonight we look at the extraordinary career of myself, one of the giants of contemporary literature. In particular, we'll be promoting my new novel, *Dancing All The Way To The Bank*. Now this remarkable novel has been turned into a brilliant television series, thanks to an innovative adaptation by one of the most promising screen-writers of the age, myself. And here to advertise — I'm sorry, analyse — this major cultural event is Melvyn Barg.

(Cut to windswept man striding over huge mountains of money)

BARG *(for it is he):* Ever since I was a lad, I have loved these rolling green hills of pound notes. In my book I tell the story of how a middleaged man falls passionately in love with himself, and then seduces the BBC into giving him stacks of cash.

(Cut to violent pornographic rape scene which lasts for ten minutes. Cut away to two men sitting in BBC office watching same rape scene on video)

J. BIRT: Cor, this is steamy stuff, Melve. I don't remember it from the book.

BARG: Don't be daft, John, 'appen it's not in the book, tha' stoopid wazzock.

BIRT: Good thinking, Melve, 'cos the rest of the book was pretty dull, to say the least.

BARG: Don't tha' tell me what's what. Me, I'm bloody intellectual, I am. I'm boss of flagship arts programme, tha' knows.

BIRT *(impressed):* Well, when I said it was dull, Melve, I didn't mean all the leg-over stuff. That's brilliant. Just what the BBC's looking for.

BARG: And what's more, my novel has been compared by Clive James, no less, to Nabonkov's *Loadsalolly* and D.H. Lawrence's *Lady Windermere's Fanny*.

(Birt hands over enormous cheque. Cut to Melvyn Bragg [played by Ronald Cockup] walking into branch of the Bank of Cumbria. WARNING: some viewers may find what follows distasteful. It involves explicit scenes of Melvyn Barg depositing a large sum of money in the bank)

MISS FROBISHER
(placing cup of tea on bank manager's desk): Good morning, Mr Chequecard. I've got Mr Barg outside. He's absolutely gasping to give it to you.

BANK MANAGER
(trembling): I can hardly wait. Could you leave us alone, please, Miss Frobisher? We've got to get down to it right away.

(Enter tousle-haired Cumbrian television personality. Romantic music swells to climax)

BARG *(breathing heavily):* I've never done this before. I don't know what to say. I don't know what to do.

(Takes fat cheque out of trousers in slow motion)

CHEQUECARD *(eyes boggling):* Good grief, I've never seen one that big before. It's the biggest I've ever seen.

BARG: You know what the great Cumbrian poet William Wordsworth wrote?

CHEQUEBOOK: No, no, Melvyn. Stop. Don't say anything. Just get on with it. You won't regret it.

BARG: Alright, alright. Here it is.

(Hands over cheque to bank manager, who faints in ecstasy. Cut back to Melvyn in LWT studio)

BARG: So there you have it, a work of genius and no mistake. That's all from *The South Bonk Show* this week, but don't forget — this programme will be discussed on tomorrow's *Start The Week* with guests Melvyn Barg, Ronald Cockup and myself.

(Viewers continue to watch video of Gremlins II)

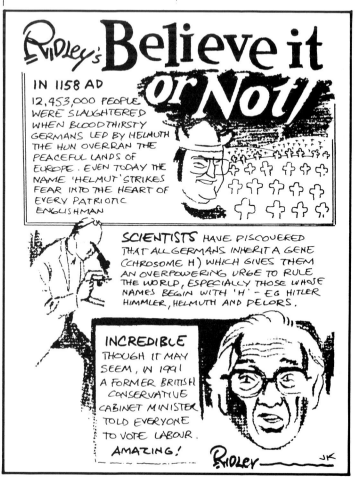

Christmas TV Films

Christmas Day
4.00pm BBC2

Au Revoir les Viewers (b&w, 1hr 27mins). Classic 1923 French masterpiece by director Pierre d'Or. Shown for the first time on television, this sombre even-paced *filme verité* tells the story of a young boy's discovery of how boring French films were during the 1920s. With Caroline St Michele, and the young Jean Birt as the boy.

Eye Rating: Z-z-z-z

Christmas Day
9.00pm BBC1

Fatman (MGN, colour, 7hrs). Multi-million-pound extravaganza which was successfully adapted from the cartoon characters that ran in a daily newspaper — Fatman and Robbing.

By day Fatman was successful entrepreneur, philanthropist and publisher Robert Maxwell. By night he stole millions of pounds and put them in his own pocket. Starring Robert Morley as Fatman and Kevin Maxwell as "The Boy Wondering-if-he's-going-to-chokey".

Eye Rating: Don't miss him at all.

Boxing Day Evening
10.00pm ITV

Clint Eastwood double bill — *Every Which Way He's On* and *Fistful of Repeats*. Two vintage Clint Eastwood films from the '70s, shown for the very 38th time on television. No need to remind you of the plot — you must know it backwards by now, especially that bit where, you know, he shoots the rope from round whatsit's neck, Lee Van Cleef or the other one.

Eye Rating: Brilliant. Five stars.

New Year's Eve
9.00pm BBC2

Le Grand Ennui (b&w, 1hr). The season of French masterpieces continues with Jean Rapideau's highly acclaimed 1931 portrayal of a family over Christmas desperately looking for something to watch on television. In a tragic climax, the father (played by Gerard Ronson) storms out of the house and goes to the video shop.

Eye Rating: Z-z-z-z-z.

New Year's Day Evening
3.20pm ITV

They Danced To Bruges (colour, 150mins)
1953 Hollywood remake of the classic English World War Two film *They Flew To Bruges*, a long-time Christmas favourite with viewers.

The transformation to full-scale musical works perfectly, with Frank Sinatra excelling as Squadron-Leader P.K. "Pinky" Braithwaite, who leads the victorious all-dancing assault on the sleepy occupied town of Bruges. The cast is a galaxy of Hollywood giants, including Gene Kelly as Group Captain "Spiffy" Wilkington, Dean Martin as Gunner Jock "Jock" MacSporran, Doris Day as Wren officer Betty Carruthers, and Marilyn Monroe, who pops up as the Lady Mayoress of Bruges. The spectacular tap sequence in the divisional headquarters of the Waffen SS to Normy Schwarzkopf's hit *We're Dancing to Bruges* is quite unforgettable.
(That's enough terrible films. Ed.)

HALO
MARY AND JOSEPH INVITE US INTO THE STABLE TO SHARE IN THE JOY OF THE BIRTH OF THEIR SON.

GLENDA SLAGG

Fleet Street's Floppy Dish

HAT'S OFF to Paddy Ashdown, the Lib-Lab Lothario from sizzling Somerset!?!

Who cares if Pantin' Paddy had a fling with his typist!?!?

What hot-blooded male with an eye for the gals doesn't like a bit on the side!?!

Passionate Paddy gets my vote any day of the week?!?

Here's to a well-hung Parliament!!?! (Geddit?!?)

WHO does he think he is, Mr Paddy So-called Ashdown?!?! Just because he's leader of the Lib-Dems doesn't mean he can go a-squeezin' and a-sleazin' with the dame who types his letters?!?

Get on back to the Missus, Mr Bonk-Happy!?!

You won't be getting any of Glenda's X's on your ballot paper!?!

TOWELS OFF to Yasser Arafat!?! (Aunty Glenda's li'l joke!?!)

He's the 60-year-old PLO terrorist with the designer stubble who set the world alight with his bombs!!?

Now yummy Mr Yasser is throwing in the towel and taking to a pretty little piece initiative half his age?!? (Geddit?!)

Good on yer, Yasser!?! Or, as he might say, "Yasser, she's my baby?!?"

HATS OFF to Bonkin' Bill Clinton! He's the Dirty Democrat who [Take in first two pars].

READ The Oldie yet??!??! Forgeddit!!?!

HERE they are — Glenda's Christmas Hamper Hunks of the Month!?!

RUUD LUBBERS. He's the handsome Hollander who's rockin' 'em all in the aisles at Maastricht. I wouldn't mind setting my Dutch Cap at him any day?!? Geddit?

KEVIN AND IAN MAXWELL. Two's company, but three's lots of fun?!?? Geddit?

MANGOSUTU BUTHELEZI. Crazy name, crazy guy??!?

Byeeeeeeee!!!

John Cole's Election Round-Up

Hondootedly Mostah Meejor Speculation Reaching Fever-Pitch ursa minor fortyniner excavating for a mine zippity-doo-da zebedee magic roundabout Mostah Kinnock On The Ropes jasminum nudiflorum silicone implant sinclair-stevenson faschings vank auf wien Mostah Lamont Bodget Cards Close To Chest reverend w. awdry andrea mantegna lord palumbo christopher columbus National Insurance Threshold Labour Bombshell Mostah Chris Patten shake'n'vac serendipity hot diggety peugeot the lion goes from strength to strength Mostah Roy Hattersley moicheal ignatieff pizzicato polka Likelihood Of Hung Parliament Olster Unionists Hold Tromp Card hugh montgomery massingberd thank goodness I'm retiring *(Cont. p. 94)*

BCCI creditor to be paid in full

by Our City Correspondent
Fred Needle

ONE BCCI creditor is to be paid in full, the official liquidator announced last night.

Champagne corks popped in EC3 as the news came through that the liquidator had managed to discover sufficient funds to pay himself.

Call Touche Ross

"I am delighted," he told his wife on the phone. "I'll be back on the 7.23 and we'll go out to celebrate at that new French place in Esher."

"That's the man you're looking for, Officer"

HANZ-Z-Z-ARD

Question Time.   2.30pm

Sir Bufton Tufton (Lymeswold, Con): In view of the forthcoming election, does the Prime Minister agree that the Labour Party's tax proposals would cause mass starvation in the capital this winter?

Mr John Major (Job-on-Lyne, Con) *(leaping to feet holding clipboard):* Yes sir. No sir. Three bags full, sir.

(Tory cheers, Labour boos)

Mr Neil Windbag (Flannelly, Lab): Could the Right Honourable Gentleman, the Prime Minister, tell the House just why it is that, according to the latest figures published by the independent analysts Goldsack Winebar, the average annual rate of growth across the Community has been consistently *(looks hard at scrap of paper and tries to read John Smith's handwriting)* 3.6 per cent higher than achieved in the last three years by this discredited, disintegrating and disgraceful government?

(Labour cheers and cries of "Has he finished the question yet?")

Mr John Major *(leaping nimbly to feet):* Yes sir. No sir. Three bags full, sir.

(Wild Tory cheers)

Mr Paddington Ashtray *(Weevil, Lib-Dem.-Bones-Dem-Bones):* As a former Royal Marine, I would just like to deplore the pathetic inter-party sniping that has so far characterised this election campaign. I hereby give a pledge that we in the Liberal-Democratic Party would never sink so low as to engage in the kind of childish name-calling displayed by the leaders of the two main parties, the faceless twit Major and the flatulent fool Kinnock.

(Lib-Dem cheer)

Mr Peter Brooke (Foot-in-Mouth, Con): I would like to offer my deepest and most sincere apologies to the House for my tactless and insensitive singing of the song *Clementine* on the Dublin television show *Gay Chatline* at 2.30 last Wednesday morning. I now realise that this was a very grievous error of judgement, and I would like to offer my resignation to the Prime Minister.

(Tory MPs take out onions in mass display of grief-struck hypocrisy)

Mr J. Major *(banging clipboard on dispatch box):* I would like to refer my honourable friend to my previous answer: Yes sir. No sir. Three bags full, sir.

Rev Ian Looney (Paisley, Ulster Democratic Anti-Papist Unionist): The Secretary of State has been guilty of a most heinous and mortal crime against the whole people of the province of Northern Ireland. In all the history of outrages that have stained the bloodstained pages of the annals of our sad and troubled land, there is no single act of criminal barbarity to compare with the cowardly singing of *Clementine* on the *Gay Switchboard Show*.

(Runs across floor of House and attempts to attack Brooke with heavy leatherbound volume of King William III Bible)

Sir Creepy Crawley *(Seat-Under-Threat, Con):* May I just say that we on the Government benches fully appreciate and understand the very real feelings of outrage expressed by the Rev Looney, whose opinions and indeed support we might be in a position to value so greatly in the event of a hung parliament when we are ten seats short?

(House empties as members run to nearest bar at thought of Paisley holding balance of power)

The Daily Hellograph

The Press And Prurience

THE most disturbing feature of what will inevitably become known as "The Ashdown Affair" has not been the behaviour of the Member for Yeovil himself but rather the highly questionable role played in this whole unhappy business by certain sections of the popular press. No one would maintain that a politician's private life should be entirely above scrutiny. Yet the fact that an MP should have had a brief sexual liaison with his secretary a long time ago cannot possibly constitute a legitimate subject for interest by the press. The salacious and prurient coverage of this particular story by the tabloid papers has marked a new low point in the history of British journalism. Readers have not been spared a single aspect of this sorry story... tasteless... titillatory... renews case for Invasion of Privacy Bill... crying need to put house in order... day when Fleet Street should hang its head in shame.

There's Moore Fun In The Daily Telegraph!

THATCHILL THE FINAL YEARS

The concluding part of Martin Gilbert's much-acclaimed, award-winning documentary series on Britain's greatest wartime leader.

(Elgar-style music composed by Andrew, Lord Webber. Shot of boring-looking man in glasses sitting in library)

MARTIN GILBERT *(for it is he)*: In 1945 the British people decisively rejected the leader who had brought them to victory in three world wars.

(Film of tearful Mrs Thatcher leaving Downing Street. Shot of ageing thug leaning on farm gate)

LORD INGHAM OF LEAK: It was a black moment when I had to tell Margaret what had happened. She just couldn't believe it. She cried and I don't mind admitting that I had a bit of a blub too *(takes out onion)*. She said

"After all I have done for them, the ungrateful swine."

LADY CAROL THATCHER: Mummy never really came to terms with not being Supreme Ruler of the Universe. She used to wake up in the middle of the night rambling on about the great summit conferences of the past which she had organised with her friends Ronnie Roosevelt and Mikhail Stalin.

GILBERT: As decline and old age set in, Thatchill increasingly turned for solace to the consolations of literature. She began writing her now-legendary 12-volume historical work *THE THATCHER ERA ...*

(Shot of pile of huge volumes, subtitled 'The Years of Greatness', 'The Years of Success', 'The Years of Triumph', 'The Years of Lunacy', 'The Great Betrayal', etc).

MR HUGE PROFIT: I remember very well the day I first went to Chester Square to write Mrs Thatcher's memoirs for her. She gave me a big file labelled "My Greatest Speeches 1979-1990". It was an immense privilege to work with her. I can never forget how, after I had written each chapter, she would insert a short phrase such as "I was brilliant," or "Once again I was right". It was a lesson in how to write great literature.

(Breaks down in tears as onion falls from pocket and rolls across floor)

LORD HOWARTH OF BROWNTONGUE *(shurely 'shirt'? Ed)*: Towards the end I'm afraid that her judgement did rather go, and began to associate with some very unsuitable characters. It was my unhappy duty at one point to step in, to warn her that she was seeing far too much of one undesirable chap in particular.

(Film of Thatchill nodding her head as she talks to her son by swimming pool in Texas)

GILBERT: The end came suddenly, in the year 2075, when at the age of 154 Mrs Thatchill passed peacefully away, shouting: "Howe, Heseltine, Major — one day I'll get even with all of you!"

(Old black and white film of state funeral. Bells toll solemnly as cortege winds its way up Whitehall. A lone figure is seen dancing deliriously on grave in Grantham. It is the 198-year-old Lord Heath of Sourgrapes)

I SEE RUSSIANS STARVING

by Our Man In London
Lunchtime O'Booze

MARIA Madeitupovich shrugged her muscular Russian shoulders wearily. For fifteen days she had been queuing at the famous Bogusov No. 1 food store in Central Moscow, in the hope of buying a small piece of sausage to feed her 17-strong family.

But when she finally reached the front of the queue, clutching her pathetic bundle of million-rouble notes, the equivalent of an entire year's wages from her job in the Imaginari Tractor Factory, she was brusquely told by the assistant that the price of sausage had risen during the previous ten minutes to 20 trillion roubles, more than she could hope to earn in her lifetime, and anyway that the shop had not had any sausage since 1981.

As she trudged wearily back through the snow to her one-room flat on the Doesntexistski Prospekt, she shrugged her muscular Russian shoulders and said: "Yeltsin? Pah. He is finished. Things were better under Stalin. At least he made the sausages run on time." *(You're fired. Ed.)*

EYELECTION '92

■ Every minute, every hour, every day, we shall be bringing you round-the-clock news, views and snooze *(surely 'comment'? Ed)* on the parties, the leaders, the issues that make up Britain's most closely fought election for decades.

MARGINAL ROUNDUP by Marginal Proops

Neasden Central

■ Historically one of Labour's safest seats in south-east England, Neasden Central fell to the Tories in 1983 by only 256 votes. The successful candidate, Terry Towelling, a local estate agent, held the seat in 1987, increasing his majority to 25,860. But in the past two years the recession has hit Neasden hard. In the once-bustling Tesco Road shopping precinct, the Tie Rack, Sock Shop, and the Spud-u-like Sushi Takeaway Heel Bar Massage Parlour all stand closed, with FOR SALE signs in the window.

"Times are hard," says

local newsagent Monty Gerhardi. "In the good old days of Thatcherism I'd be shifting half a dozen Yorkie Bars in an afternoon. Now I'm lucky if I sell one."

It was the same story in the Gerald Ronson Karaoke Lounge of the Boston Arms. "Two years ago you couldn't get a seat in here at lunchtime. Now I'm the only person drinking."

Up the road, the once-thriving futon factory, which in the boom years employed as many as two people (Sid and Doris Bonkers), last month closed its doors for ever.

Against this background it is going to be a hard-fought contest, as Labour's Jill Gobb, a 42-year-old supply teacher, battles to wrest Neasden back to the Labour fold. "After thirteen years of Tory misrule, the people of Neasden are saying 'It's time for a change'."

Meanwhile the Lib Dems, who have been showing well in local council elections, are hoping to improve on their 1987 showing of 18.9 per cent with a strong candidate, Jocelyn Earring, 26, who is well known in the area as Chair of the Neasden Gays Against Foxhunting campaign.

But the Tory incumbent, Towelling, is undaunted by what he calls "the mountain we have to climb". As a sign that opinion is turning his way, he cites the recent meeting at the George V Memorial Hall, when

Malcolm Rifkind drew an audience of over 10 people to hear him outline Tory plans to privatise BR's parcels service.

Make no mistake, Neasden Central, 46th on Labour's target list, will be the key indicator that the rest of Britain will be watching on the night of 9 April.

Candidates in full

T. Towelling *(Con)*

J. Gobb *(Lab)*

J. Earring *(Lib Dem)*

T.H.Q. Pendleton-Smythe *(Green)*

Mandy Swishcane *(Publicity Stunt)*

Jean-Marie le Benn *(Double Whammy Raving Monster Social Democrat Party)*

H. Gussett *(Anti-Zebra Crossing)*

M. Truebeard *(Real Liberal Party)*

J. Browne *(Independent Crook)*

R. Brown *(Independent Knickers in Pocket)*

A. Hitler *(Keep Neasden White)*

Muhammed Al Jolson *(Kill Salman Rushdie Now party)*

ON THE STUMP

with Mark Beardie, Alexander Chancetogetoutoftheoffice and Everyone Else

■ At 6.30 yesterday morning I joined 3,000 other journalists on the Kinnock Express at Paddington.

Two hours later we were sitting in the St Ivel's Primary School in a suburb of Grottingham. Things were not going well for the well-oiled Walworth Road election machine. The spin doctors were visibly nervous as one microphone after another failed to work. "It's what we call a testing time," said one Kinnock aide, breaking the tension.

Eventually we were allowed to watch on closed-circuit television the Labour leader crouching down to talk to a hand-picked group of nine-year-olds. "I hope he doesn't find their questions too demanding," quipped one cynical journalist (myself).

But soon we were on our way again as the dove-grey Major battlebus swung us onto the M95, heading for the key marginal of Grotchester. Here the photo-opportunity was the sight of Mr Major in a white coat talking to selected workers in a crisp factory. "I hope you'll all be supporting us on 9 April," he told them. "Not the crispest example of election repartee," joked one weary media-wag (myself).

But already we had been whistled on our way to the old cotton town of Grochdale, in the Ashdown Helicopter.

This time we had the chance to watch the Liberal Democrat leader donning a

hard hat to tour a new multi-storey car park which is to be named after the town's former Liberal MP Sir Cyril Pavarotti.

Ashdown told his audience of journalists: "We are on our way." I'm not sure that many of us battle-weary reporters were disposed to believe him.

There is an air of total unreality about this election. One sometimes feels that it has been reduced to nothing more than a media-circus.

As the helicopter took us home to London, one hack whose wit remained undimmed by the day's experiences (myself yet again) quipped: "Good to see Paddy's got his chopper out again."

Somehow it seemed to sum up the whole election.

© *All newspapers, every day, 1992.*

TOMORROW: The same piece again.

Diana Smirk　　**Harriet Lovey**　　**John Cleese**

HOW THE STARS LINE UP FOR BRITAIN'S DAY OF DECISION

TORY

Diana Smirk *(ITV's "Mrs Fothergill")*

Fred Rabbit *(STV's "Mr Magic")*

Jimmy Jinks *(comedian)*

Sid Leafmould *(presenter of Radio Trent's The Weekend Gardener)*

Felicity Floss *(actress)*

Gary Foul *(professional footballer)*

Ken Higgit *(best-selling novelist, The Icarus Conundrum and others)*

Lucinda Lycett-Green *(finalist in Stockholm 3-Day Eventing European Cup, 1982).*

LABOUR

Harriet Lovey *(RSC actress)*

Harry Neasden *(alternative comedian)*

Len Poach *(director of Channel Four's award-winning Up The IRA drama-documentary)*

Gary Goal *(professional footballer)*

Ken Haggit *(best-selling novelist, The Daedalus Complex and others)*

Jenny Spring *(4x400 bronze medallist, Bratislava Games 1986)*

Crispin Fry *(actor, star of Neasden Building Society commercial)*

Sara Dimwit *(presenter of BBC2's late-night art show, Turn Off)*

Mrs Margaret Thatcher *(shurely shome mishtake?)*

LIB DEMS

John Cleese *(millionaire businessman).*

Reprinted from the Labour Party Manifesto

The Coming Of The Major

April was the cruellest month.
We had a hard time, with the
Poll tax and Liverpool
Getting knocked out of the UEFA Cup.

No wonder there are millions of homeless
In the streets and the latest
Unemployment figures are frankly, to my
Mind, sickening.

I blame Thatch.
And that new bloke with the glasses.
Major, Major, Major. Out, out, out.
Vote Labour on 9 April.

Adrian Spart (59¾)

Adrian Spart is a Liverpool poet published by Fabber and Fabber. His recent collection *Eliot Was A Fascist* **is available from the Toxteth Poetry Workspace, 12p.**

Have we been here before? asks Alan Watneys

■ The present election must remind us all of the dilemma which faced Lord Liverpool in 1826 when he decided to dissolve the famous "Turnip Parliament" and go to the country on the issue of the repeal of the laws against man-traps.

His Whig opponent, Sir Edward James Fox the Younger, tried to rally the opposition behind the slogan LIVERPOOL'S DOUBLE WHAMMY COULD MEAN INCOME TAX UP TO 2d. However, it was the unexpected intervention of the Hon. Kevin Cavendish-Portland (later the 14th Duke of Rutland) which (contd p.94)

"Dad, what came first — the chicken or the basket?"

EYE FORUM
by Brian Farmyard

Animal Genocide or our English way of life?

TO THE DIRTY TELEGRAPH

AGAINST

Dave Spart, Co-Chair of the Neasden Action League Against Vertebrate Holocaust.

Er, once again the British Establishment closes ranks to defend the totally sickening so-called sport of fox-hunting, i.e. a group of rich, upper-class sadists marauding around the countryside in order to murder and torture a totally innocent and defenceless animal, i.e. a fox, so that they can glory in the sight of its guts being ripped out by trained killer-dogs who have been deliberately starved for weeks to turn them into killing machines capable of chewing off a toddler's arm... er... it is totally sickening. As the great homosexual rights activist Oscar Wilde so profoundly put it: "Hunting is the totally sickening in full pursuit of the totally unacceptable."

FOR

John Nortiboys QC, playwright, barrister, bon viveur and bon voyage round my father.

Hullo. As a life-long socialist, there is nothing I find more agreeable than to stand in an Oxfordshire lane on a crisp November morning and to hear coming across the frost-encrusted fields from some distant spinney, the age-old call of the huntsman: "John, you're wanted on the phone. You can take it in my Range Rover." Oh, how thrilling, as I gallop across to the car to hear the unmistakable bark of my old friend Baroness Mallalieu inviting Penny and me over to lunch at her place, to discuss these dreadful long-haired hunt saboteurs who are trying to destroy forever the England of John Peel, John Betjeman and John Mortimer.

SIR—As a leading member of the sado-masochistic gay community, I would like to register the strongest possible protest at the decision of the Appeal Court to uphold the conviction of one of our members in the case of Regina vs S.M & Others.

As a result of this transvesty of justice, I and several like-minded persons plan to nail ourselves to the door of 10 Downing Street and encourage the police to beat us up and trample us to within an inch of our lives with their strong, majestic horses.

Sympathisers who wish to join the demonstration are advised to dress informally (black leather g-string and studded collar) and arrive at Downing Street no later than 10.69am on the morning of March 3rd.

THE MARQUIS
DE GUSSETT,
Full name, address and photographs supplied,
c/o Punch Me Magazine,
Blackleatherfriars Bridge,
London.

How the celebrities line up on the most important issue confronting humanity today

FOR	AGAINST
Barbara Cartland	Sir Nedward Sherrin
Count Nikolai Tolstoy	Sir Yehudi Menuhin
Cliff Richard	Melvyn Bragg
TV's Charles Moore	Jason Donovan
Trevor Macdonald	Robin Cook MP
Will Carling	Jane Torvill
Norman Stone	Maureen Lipman
Roger Scruton	Anita Roddick
Rod Stewart	Stephen Fry
Rod Hull and Emu	Barry Cryer
Norman Willis	Norman Willis
Barry Cryer	Rod Hull and Emu
Stephen Fry	Rod Stewart
Anita Roddick	Roger Scruton
Maureen Lipman	Norman Stone
Jane Torvill	Will Carling
Robin Cook MP	Trevor Macdonald
Jason Donovan	TV's Charles Moore
Melvyn Bragg	Cliff Richard
Sir Yehudi Menuhin	Count Nikolai Tolstoy
Sir Nedward Sherrin	Barbara Cartland

"Bloody hunt saboteurs"

BBC2 *9.00*

On Again

by Harold Pinter

(A man and a woman sit in front of a television. He is balding with glasses. She wears shiny high-heeled shoes)

SHE: You're on again.

HE: On what?

(Pause)

SHE: There. You know. Again.

HE: Am I?

(He crosses room and comes back with bowl)

HE: Would you like an olive?

(We hear an actor on the television)

ACTOR: Would you like an olive?

SHE: You're never off. Always on.

(There is a long pause. He eats the olive menacingly. We hear actress on the television)

ACTRESS: You're never off. Always on.

SHE: Shall I turn it off?

HE: He came again today.

SHE: Who? Yentob?

HE: He said I'll be on again soon.

(Very short pause as they look at the television)

SHE: There you are, you're on. Yentob said you'd be on.

HE: On what?

SHE: There, you know. Again.

(Continued indefinitely)

OBITUARIES

(reprinted from the Daily Goodbyegraph)

THE EARL OF MUSKET

The 14th Earl of Musket, always known as Algy, who died on the 13th January at the age of 98 was the last surviving great-great-grand-nephew of the Duke of Clarence. As a result, the Earldom of Musket falls into abeyance, although his Scottish Viscountcy, the Buccleuch of That Leuch, passes to his third cousin, the Hon. Ziggy Smack, who runs a travelling disco-theque.

Algy Musket inherited his title in 1937 from his grandfather, the 13th Earl, who died in a tram crash in Sydney, Australia. His great-grandfather, the 12th Earl, enjoyed a brief notoriety in the 1880s, as one of the central figures in the Tranby Croft "top hat affair", in which a practical joke involving the Prince of Wales and a goldfish went disastrously wrong.

"Double Whammy" Musket, as he was known, honourably refused to give evidence against a member of the Royal Family in the subsequent libel action, and was rewarded by Queen Victoria with the Fifedom of Fife.

His aunt, the formidable Lady Grimswade, was a legendary leg to boot in otter hunting circles, and her second husband, the 12th Duke of Ballyloony, was briefly ADC to the Governor of Malta during the 1920s, before he was tragically drowned in a boating accident off Pantellaria in 1928.

It was his sister, Lady Camomile Lycett-Green, who was thought to have provided the original model for Mrs Satterthwaite in Aldous Huxley's satirical novel *Eyeless in Gozo* (1929).

Algy Musket lived quietly in Leicestershire and never did anything at all.

(Will this do? Hugh Matey Mockingberd)

Before   After

How to get your weight down to 21-stone the Pavarotti way

Breakfast
Love of 3000 Orange Juice
The Porridge of Figaro
Madame Buttered Toast
– ✳ –
Lunch
Schubert's Smoked Trout
Coronation Chicken of Poppeia
Magic Fruit with Cosi Fan Tutti-Frutti
Ice Cream
– ✳ –
Dinner
Roll Mop Albert Herring
Caviare Rusticana
Merry Wives of Brown Windsor Soup
Tagliatelli Verdi
Death in Venison
Der Fledermousse
– ✳ –
Plus
300 Tons of Lard to be taken daily
between meals

"It works," says TV's opera-loving DAVID MELLOR

The GAMBOLLARDS
by Eve and Nick Bollard

MMM.... TALK DIRTY TO ME DARLING

LOONY LEFTY KINNOCK GAY LESBIAN TAX PLAN SMITH COMMIE UNIONS WINTER OF DISCONTENT....

OH YES! OH YES!

How they will be voting

Why I will be voting Labour

by Bertram Wooster

I'VE never been much of a political bird. So when it comes to tootling down to the polling both to put one's X on the old blotting paper, yours truly is usually found heading off with a hamper in the opposite direction.

However, of late, my man Jeeves has become curiously one-track on the crying need, as he puts it, to give this Kinnock cove a crack at being top banana. According to Jeeves, we members of the well-heeled fraternity have had it plushy for far too long, and it is time to plunge our jolly old hands into the washbucket and shell out a thickish wad of the folding stuff to help our under-privileged brethren.

"But dash it all, Jeeves," I said to him. "There's not much incentive for a chap to work if he has to hand over every hard-earned penny to the un-washed."

"But, sir," he retorted. "It does have to be admitted, with the greatest respect, sir, that you yourself do not actually, in the accepted sense of the term, work."

"By jove, Jeeves, you're absolutely right. How was it that Latin johnny of yours put it?"

" 'Rem acu tetigisti', I believe, sir, is the expression you are endeavouring to recall."

I was so bowled over by the full force of his logic that I am fully resolved, come April 10th, to bung my vote in the direction of our local Socialist candidate, Comrade Sid Stoad.

© Stephen Fry, Daily Telegraph

"Someone thinks the recession is over"

Why I will be voting Labour

by Margaret Thatcher

MY decision to vote Labour at this election dates back to a day in November 1990. It was then that I realised in a blinding flash that the Conservative Party was completely finished as an effective political force. They had turned their back on everything they had once believed in — i.e. myself. Bastards! They deserve everything that's coming to them, particularly that slimy little creep in glasses who I always warned would be a disaster. Vote Labour. Get rid of all of them and bring back me.

Modern Miracles
No. 94

The Holy Spring of Saunders

In 1992 there occurred the only known case of spontaneous recovery from Alzheimer's Disease. An elderly man believed to be near death drank of the waters at the fountain of Ford Open Prison in Sussex. Immediately he recovered all his former powers. A day later he was playing tennis and making plans to start a car-phone business called Out of the Cellnet plc. Warders were amazed when the man they called "The Living Corpse" walked unaided from the prison, laughing heartily and completing the *Times* crossword in less than a minute.

As a result, hundreds of in-form pilgrims now flock to the Holy Spring to sip the waters but so far, disappointingly, no one else has been cured at all.

VIEWERS PROTEST AS SOAP STARS SPLIT

By Our Soap Staff **Henry Persil and Daz Wilson**

MILLIONS of angry viewers jammed the switchboard of Buckingham Palace last night to register complaints over the latest episode of the long-running TV series *Coronation Street*.

Earlier viewers had seen two of the younger members of the cast, Andy Windsor and his wife Fergie, deciding on an "amicable separation" only a few episodes after they had been seen getting married.

Their "wedding episode" in 1986 topped that year's ratings as one of the most popular soap marriages, and was watched by an estimated 800 million people worldwide.

In recent episodes the scriptwriters have shown the couple involved in a series of marital disputes and hinted at an off-screen romance with a mysterious Texan oilperson, J.R. Hartley.

WestEnders

But it had always been assumed that the couple would be seen getting back together to keep the story-line upbeat.

The latest twist caught viewers unawares. Many of them had tuned in to last night's episode expecting to see the latest developments in the sub-plot involving Andrew's father becoming a Greek Orthodox hermit.

Instead they saw distressing scenes of lawyers haggling over the divorce settlement.

The Duke of Edinburgh says:

'Save these marriages'

"If we do not act quickly to save these magnificent marriages, the whole Royal Family will soon be extinct."

Send donations to The Duke of Edinburgh, Hon. President of The Royal Society For The Prevention of Royal Divorce

Fergie's Cashin

An agent for the red-haired actress last night issued a brief statement on her behalf which read: "I do not wish to be typecast. If you stay in a soap like this for too long people assume it's all you can do. I have my career to think of."

CAST IN FULL

Prince Andrew	HUGH LAURIE
Duchess Fergiana	VANESSA REDGRAVE
The Queen	MAUREEN LIPMAN
Duke of Edinburgh	ZORBA THE GREEK
Major Ron	GEORGE COLE
J.R. Ewing	L.P. HARTLEY

Grim Fairy Tales

Once upon a time there was a handsome prince, who was wise, clever and loved by all his people. However, he's not in this story. This is the tale of Prince Charmless.

One day he was walking through his kingdom when he chanced upon a Ferg.

And, to his amazement, the Ferg spoke. "Give us a kiss, big boy, and I'll turn into a princess."

So the Prince kissed the Ferg. And soon they were married.

But she never turned into a princess. And they lived unhappily ever after.

PETER McLIE

The World's Worst Columnist

I SEE Fergie has got a "quickie" divorce from the dashing Captain Phillips.

About time too! Whatever the fuddy-duddies may say, there is no longer any stigma about divorce. Why should we expect the Royals to behave any better than ourselves?

I say good luck to her!

☐ WE read that Princess Anne is trying to keep her marriage together.

Thank goodness someone is, in these days of quickie divorces.

We have a right to expect the Royal Family to set an example by behaving better than the rest of us.

I say good luck to her!

☐ *WHOEVER invented shoelaces deserves a medal in my opinion.*

Just imagine a world without these ingenious little lengths of string.

Why — one's shoes would fall off constantly, as one walked along the street. It would take hours to get anywhere at all.

Britain's inventors have a great deal to be proud of, wouldn't you say?

☐ WALKING through the streets I have noticed a number of people with furry, four-legged creatures trotting along beside them, usually attached to a piece of string.

What is this absurd new fashion, I would like to know?

The next thing we know, people will be putting little red fish into bowls!

Isn't life grand?

(You're fired. Ed.)

Tales from HisTory Central Office No. 94

PILGRIMS FLOCK TO WEMBLEY FOR EASTER MESSAGE

by Our Religious Staff **David Bowie-Our-Heads-In-Prayer**

Millions of pilgrims from all over the world frocked *(shurely 'flocked'? Ed)* to Wembley yesterday to hear the traditional Easter message from the Pop.

On easter Monday, or the Feast of St Frederick of Mercury, as it is more correctly known, the assembled worshippers heard a series of messages from some of the most religious figures in sex, drugs and rock and roll.

St George Michael and the Drag Act

"Freddie is not dead but lives on through his music," preached the Very Reverend Elizabeth Taylor. "He is with us tonight," spake Her Grace Annie Lennox. "Don't forget he was absolutely divine," intoned His Holiness Elton John.

The Loafers and the Fishnets

During the seven-hour service, beamed by satellite to billions of the faithful all over the world, the congregation sang hymns associated with St Frederick such as *I Want It Now, We Are The Champions* and the deeply spiritual *Bohemian Rhapsody* with its moving concluding final verse "Nothing really matters to me."

In a dedication to the life and work of St Frederick a number of miracles were performed, including the resurrection of Liza Minnelli and the late Roger Daltrey from the Whohe.

Sir Robert Geldof is 40.

BUSH TO VISIT AMERICA

by Our Los Angeles Staff
Martin Looter King

PRESIDENT BUSH today announced that he would shortly be paying a visit to war-torn America.

"I sent the troops in," he told newsmen. "Now I think it's probably safe for me to see what's happening."

Questioned by reporters, the President said: "America still has a duty to maintain peace in the world, even in America."

Vote For Burning Bush

"We are not going to be pushed around by ourselves," he said. "I have told our boys to get in there and kick heads *(shurely 'ass'? Ed)*.

"America can hold her head up high and say that we won. And lost."

Mr Bush then burst into song with his rendition of the new National Anthem:

*Oh say can't you see
By the dawn's early light
Isn't that Los Angeles being
 burned to the ground?
Oh what a lootiful morning*

(continued page 94)

WHAT THE L.A. JURY SAW

Easter TV Choice

Joan Bakewell Tart interviews a controversial Church of England priest who believes in God.

BAKEWELL: So you believe that Christ was in some way God?

PRIEST: Yes.

BAKEWELL: Don't you think your congregation would be very shocked if they knew that?

PRIEST: Well, yes, but nowadays, you know, things are different; there is more tolerance towards minority views like mine.

BAKEWELL: You believe in the Resurrection, don't you?

PRIEST: Er, I suppose I do really.

BAKEWELL: Many of your parishioners might find that offensive.

PRIEST: Well, I hope I have the support of my bishop.

BISHOP OF DURHAM *(for it is he)*: No you don't. You're fired.

BAKEWELL: Goodnight and God bless.

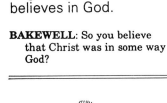

PRIVATISED TRAIN SET

THE Sun

FRIDAY, APRIL 24, 1992   25p

BUGGER OFF YOU BALD BASTARD!

by Kelvin McFilth

NEIL KINNOCK is trying to make out that the Sun conducted a campaign against him and made him lose the election.

Wot a load of bollox, quite frankly. Admittedly, we urged our readers to vote Conservative but, as none of them can read, it is absurd to suggest that anything we write can influence them in any way. We have always been totally fair to Kinnock, despite his being a KGB homosexual childkiller and a Welsh wanker to boot. So shut your gob, boyo, and get your facts right.

On other pages

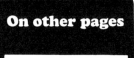

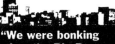
How we had nothing to do with it. The Sun's headline yesterday which proves Kinnock is lying

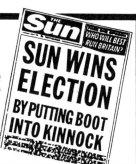

THE Sun   WHO WILL BEST RUN BRITAIN?
SUN WINS ELECTION BY PUTTING BOOT INTO KINNOCK

In The Courts

The Case of Jason P. Dreamcoat vs *The Fuck* Magazine

The case continued today before Mr Justice Cocklecarrot. Appearing for Mr Dreamcoat, Sir Charles Greyman QC said that his client was one of the most distinguished actors of his generation, known throughout the world for his portrayal of Wayne Billabong in the Australian soap *The Cobbers*.

COCKLECARROT: What is an soap?

GREYMAN: M'lud, it is a type of popular entertainment on the televisual device with regular episodes repeated throughout the week.

COCKLECARROT: Thank you, Mr Greyman. Pray continue.

GREYMAN: More recently my client Mr Dreamboat has played the leading role in one of Mr Andrew Lloyd Webber's musical masterpieces, *Jason And The Golden Fleecing The Public*.

COCKLECARROT: Who is Andrew Lloyd Webber?

(Laughter)

GREYMAN: Ladies and gentlemen and gays on the jury should there so be, I draw your attention now to bumble bee.

COCKLECARROT: The word is 'bundle', is it not?

(More laughter)

GREYMAN: As Your Lordship pleases.

COCKLECARROT: It pleases me a great deal.

(Paroxysms of laughter from whole court)

GREYMAN: Be so good as to examine the issue of *The Fuck* magazine, number 94 I believe, in which my client is portrayed in an T-shirt bearing the slogan VOTE CONSERVATIVE. We submit that there can be no greater libel to any man's reputation than this disgraceful smear.

(Sir Hartley Redface, representing The Fuck, then began his cross-examination)

REDFACE: I put it to you, Mr Showboat, that you are not as other men.

SHOWBOAT: I resent that deeply. I have nothing against the Gay Community and indeed I have the highest respect for their lifestyle. However, I won't be called a filthy old queen by anyone. Do I make myself clear?

REDFACE: Do you deny voting Conservative?

SHOWTRIAL: What I do in the privacy of my own voting booth is no concern of anyone else's.

COCKLECOTTAGE: Is your hair naturally that yellow shade, young man?

SHOWDOWN: Not entirely, Your Honour. I use lemon juice, which gives it a lovely blond tint.

COCKLEBUGGER: So your case, Mr Redface, could be summed up, could it not, by the popular expression "Blonds do not prefer gentleman"?

(Three-day recess as court recovers from laughter at judicial bon mot)

The judge then summed up the case, advising the jury not to award Mr Dreamcoat damages of more than "the cost of a pair of trousers".

FOREMAN: £200,000 and an autograph, please.

The case and the magazine then ended

The Daily Telegraph

PERSONAL VIEW

CHRISTOPHER BARKWORTH

The dark shadow over us all

ON APRIL 9th an extraordinary thing happened. Whilst all the experts were predicting a Labour victory, I took a stroll down our village high street, where I met Mrs Fothergill, the sub-postmistress.

"Lovely day, Mr Barkworth," she said. "Let's not spoil it by voting Labour." Everywhere the story was the same. My friend Mr Waldegrave told me that he was going to vote Conservative. As did Sir Marmalade Gussett, a recluse who lives nearby. Why was it that all these ordinary people suddenly decided to fly against all the indications of a Kinnock triumph?

I believe that at the last minute a dark cloud suddenly appeared over the nation's collective unconscious. And that dark cloud of socialism casting its baleful shadow over every aspect of British life could only be dispelled by affirming the Jungian positive and voting Conservative, thereby saving about £6,000 a year in my own case *(shurely 'saving the nation from the nightmare phase of the left-wing dream'? Ed).*

NUREMBURG RALLY A MISTAKE SAYS HITLERSLEY

by Our Propaganda Staff
Josef Gerbils and Joseph Haines

THE Deputy Führer of the Labour Party, Herr Hittersley, today conceded that, in retrospect, the Nuremburg Rally could now be seen to have been a mistake. "At the time it seemed a good idea — but it may have given the impression that we had already won the war," said Hittersley.

The notorious rally was brilliantly stage-managed, with tens of thousands of loyal Party actors cheering the Leader, to the strains of German music, while searchlights picked out the party's High Command as they strutted across the stage, punching the air and prophesying total victory.

No Herr Kinnock

Today Herr Hitlersley admits that this one evening cost the Labour Party the chance to rule for a thousand years.

THE BIG BORE THEORY EXPLAINED

For *Private Eye* readers, a unique guide to the mystery of the universe. Here's how it works.

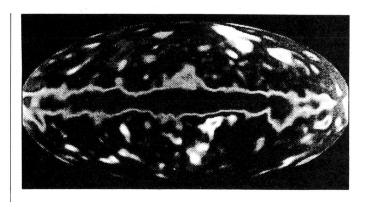

1. Originally there is no theory at all. A complete vacuum. Nothingness.

2. Then suddenly, from nowhere, Big Bore happens. men in glasses are simultaneously hurled into studios at incredible speed all over the galaxy.

3. Chaotic theories swirl out of control and hot air circulates wildly.

4. Empty space in newspapers is miraculously filled by positive "articles".

5. These are balanced by negative "articles" from Bishops.

6. For three seconds it is all mildly interesting.

7. From then it grows increasingly duller, quickly reaching a point of infinite boredom and continuing for what feels like 15 billion years.

8. You put down the newspaper and turn off your television.

9. Instead you watch an old video of *Inspector Morse*, you know, the one with Geoffrey Palmer or that other one where he goes to Australia or well any of them really except the one about the scientist…

10. Er…

11. That's it.

© TV's Patrick Bore, Professor Stephen Bawking, the Telegraph's Adrian Borey and lots of men whom you never see on the front page.

THE WORLD'S GREATEST COMIC! BENNY HILL'S IMMORTAL LEGACY OF LAUGHTER CAN NOW BE YOURS FOR ONLY 2p

Choose any three of these classic video-sketches and get 100 free, to remind you of the funniest man in the history of the world — Frankie Howerd *(shurely 'Benny Hill'? Ed)*.

Benny's Knockers
Benny as gormless postman knocks on a door which is answered by 20 girls in suspenders who chase him down the street.

Have You Had Yours Today, Madam?
Benny is the gormless milkman who delivers to a nudist colony by mistake. He is chased by 20 girls in suspenders.

Benny's Big Bang
Benny as the gormless foreman in a fireworks factory. Trouble starts when his trousers fall down and he is chased by 20 girls in suspenders.

The Lady With The Clamp
Benny as the gormless meter maid tries to put a parking ticket on an ambulance, but gets quite a surprise when 20 nurses in suspenders jump out and chase him down the street.

"The greatest clown of the twentieth century" – **Michael Ignatieff**

"Benny's genius transcends mime, theatre and the whole tradition of the commedia dell'arte" – **Jonathan Miller**

"A cultural icon of the first magnitude" – **Dr George Steiner**

"Both a surreal visual farceur and a subversive reinterpreter of the possibilities of language" – **Toby Young, The Modern Review**

(That's enough. Ed.)

OZYTHATCHIAS

By Percy Bysshe Sparty

I met a traveller on the Jubilee line
Who said: A vast tower of concrete
Stands in the Docklands. Near it lie
Idle cranes and empty offices.
And on the pedestal these words appear:
"My name is Ozythatchias,
Supreme Ruler of the Universe.
Look on my works, ye mighty, and despair."
Nothing beside remains. Round the decay
Of that colossal wreck, boundless and bare,
The lone and level sand and cement
Mixers stretch far away.

Police to become accountable — Inspector Morse sacked

by Our Crime Staff
P.C. James

A SENIOR inspector in the Thames Valley CID has become the first victim of the government's new plans to improve police efficiency.

Inspector Morse, 54, has been removed from his post on the grounds of incompetence and replaced by the newly promoted Inspector "Robbie" Lewis, 47.

Said Lewis: "Morse was increasingly solving cases by luck rather than deduction. He was becoming erratic, more emotionally involved, and revealing more about his private life every time."

Morse's record in homicide had been subject to queries for some time. Said an anonymous fat senior officer — you know, the one in the office:

"He was mostly solving the wrong cases. It was all red herrings. By the time he found the killer, another five people would have died. Sometimes he was baffled for as long as two hours."

Police are now keen to stress the importance of patient, routine police work along the ex-Sergeant-Lewis lines, rather than beer-drinking, opera-loving, womanising, Jaguar-driving, crossword-solving (*That's enough Morse. Ed.*)

O&Y STILL CONFIDENT OVER BABEL PROJECT

by Our Property Correspondent **Ozzy Mandias**

THE world's largest-ever commercial property project, the so-called Tower of Babel, will be finished on schedule, the builders pledged last night.

Their optimistic statement comes after growing speculation that the two-billion shekel project would have to be abandoned after the Brothers Reichmann admitted that they were going bust.

Oh Noah, Not Again

The project was originally launched 3,000 years ago in the time of the legendary ruler Queen Magi, who wished to commemorate her reign by seeing the world's tallest tower rise on the banks of the Thames.

It had been hoped that thousands of merchants would rush out to buy space in the Babel Tower, but, when the day came, the only takers were an eccentric band

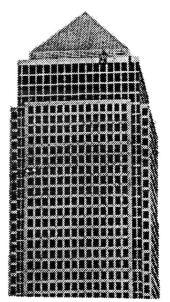

of scribes calling themselves the *Daily Telegraph*.

ROBERT THOMPSON

"You may search far and wide, but you'll never find the right bags to fit your hoover"

HURD AND MAJOR

by P. G. Wodehouse

(Saxophone music)

MAJOR *(sitting in armchair reading Daily Telegraph)*: I say, Hurd, what's this Bosnia Hercegovina business all about? Dashed complicated, what?

HURD *(polishing teapot)*: Not altogether, sir. To anyone familiar with the unhappy history of the Balkans, the situation is only too comprehensible.

MAJOR: But, dash it, Hurd, who are all these johnnies who seem to be so keen on bumping each other off all over the place — Serbs, Croats, Moslems, Bosnians? And what about the Hercegovinians? No one ever seems to mention them.

HURD: Indeed, sir, it does seem a curious oversight.

MAJOR: But, dash it all, Hurd, we can't just sit around while these birds take pot shots at each other.

HURD: Indeed we can't, sir. It is a most unfortunate state of affairs.

MAJOR: So you mean, Hurd, someone should step in at once? Friend Bush, for example? Or even yours truly?

HURD: Oh no, sir. That would be most unwise. I would strongly advise against any precipitate action of any kind in this matter, sir.

MAJOR: So you mean I don't do anything at all?

HURD: On the contrary, sir. You must do something at once.

MAJOR: Well, what?

HURD: You must tell everyone that something must be done at once.

MAJOR: Do you know, Hurd, you're a bally genius? I've always said it. It must be all that fish you keep eating or something. Do you think if I ate as much fish as you I could be a bally genius too?

HURD: I'm afraid, sir, that I very much doubt it.

MAJOR: Oh well, jolly good, Hurd. I'd better tootle down to the Drones for a spot of lunch with Oofy Mellor.

The End

NEXT EPISODE: Hurd explains sanctions.

PRISONS — NEW CRISIS

by Our Home Affairs Staff
Belmarsh Mooney

THE PRISON service was reeling last night after a shock report which forecasts that Britain's jails will soon be suffering from severe undercrowding.

This comes in the wake of the Guildford Four, Birmingham Six, Maguire Seven, M62, Royaume Uni douze points, Ireland dix points, thank you Malmo *(That's enough Eurovision Song Contest. Ed.)*

With approximately 800 further cases of miscarriage of justice waiting to be heard, the report concludes that by 1997 there will be an unacceptable ratio of "none-to-a-cell" in many prisons.

The Government is now under pressure to start knocking down prisons in order to cope with the lack of demand. Prison officers are worried that they will be "unable to deal with the shortage in numbers".

Said one: "There is going to be a crisis in the prison service unless something drastic is done."

He continued: "There are hundreds of guilty policemen wandering the streets. Why can't they be put in here?"

New exhibition by Margaritte

This is not a prime minister

Margaritte

THE extraordinary surrealist world of Margaritte has a power to shock even now, *writes George Melly yet again.* In perhaps her best-known and most controversial work, *Ce n'est pas un Prime Minister*, Margaritte Thatcher captures the inherent contradictions between what seems to be a Prime Minister and yet what is no more than a representation, a shadow, a con-trick. Working firmly in the non-European tradition *(contd page 94).*

THOUSANDS INVADE PEACEFUL VILLAGE SHOCK

by Our Music Staff **Lyn Barber of Seville**

VILLAGERS of a sleepy Sussex hamlet are up in arms at the annual invasion of a patch of local ground by thousands of so-called "music-lovers".

For the past weeks the convoys of people have been arriving at Glyndebourne from all over Britain, blocking the narrow lanes and causing havoc to local residents.

Said one outraged villager: "They are not music-lovers at all. Most of them come here to get drunk and fall asleep. They sit around on the grass with their hampers, guzzling their booze with the music blaring out."

Magic Champagne Flute

Said the local vicar: "We are kept awake every night by the sound of car doors slamming, champagne corks popping and upper-class people singing arias very badly. The police just stand by, saying: "Good evening, Sir, can I park your car for you?"

Call Nick Rossini

However, landowner George Christie, who every year lets the travellers in, said: "They are perfectly harmless — at least until the interval. Some of them do get a bit aggressive during *The Electrification of the Soviet Union* and ask for their money back, but on the whole they pose no threat."

Who are they, the so-called ravers?

Lucinda Prior-Engagement, 19: "This is my first time and I love it. The trees, the sheep, the flowers. It's nature in tune with like everything. And all my schoolfriends are here as well. It's brilliant."

David Mellor, 42, Chelsea fan and Minister for Heritage: "I'll be honest. I come here for the birds, the booze and the Bizet. You can't beat it. And what's more it's totally free. For me, anyway."

Sir Edward Heath is typical of the older generation. "Hello. There is a great atmosphere here. Of course it's no place for philistines like Mrs Thatcher. Some of the conductors are quite good, though not as good as myself."

Nathaniel "Nat" Westminster, 43, a merchant banker: "The majority of us here do very little in the winter. We just live for the summer when we can put on our fancy gear and catch the 12.43 from Victoria. I cannot understand the fuss, or indeed the operas."

HUGE GAS ERUPTION THREATENS PLANET

by our man in Rio
Lunchtime O'Zone

THE FUTURE of the planet was threatened yesterday when a vast emission of hot air began to erupt at the Earth summit in Rio de Janeiro.

Scientists blamed the sudden release of the gas on thousands of politicians and civil servants from all over the world, simultaneously demanding that something should be done, but not by them.

One principal source of the toxic rubbish was George Bush, who emitted a colossal 78 billion cubic hectares of lethal fumes in the course of a ten minute speech.

Gas-Burning Bush

According to one eye witness: "It was terrible. The planet will never recover. He opened his mouth and this stuff just came out."

Analysis of the contents of the Presidential emission revealed a quantity of Bushshit (*shurely*

'Bullshit'? Ed) well above the permitted level. There were also strong traces of Hokum, Flannel, Cowardice, Soft Soap, Electioneering, Stupidity and Monosodium Glutamate.

Bush, however, was not the only offender, with over three thousand other sources contributing to the huge mushroom cloud above Rio which environmentals warn is threatening to do nothing at all at any stage.

"Been on the market long?"

THE FUNDAY TIMES

19 JUNE 1992   Price 80p

Grave Constitutional Crisis Rocks Fairyland Over Funday Times Revelations

**by Our Royalty Staff
Enid Blyton and Hans Christian Marriage**

THE Funday Times's shock revelation that Prince Charming and his lovely bride did *not* live happily ever after, as revealed in last week's shock issue of the Funday Times, has exploded a time bomb under the whole edifice of the Fairyland monarchy.

Passages from the book *Sleeping Beauty — Her True Story*, published last week for the first time in the Funday Times, revealed to the world for the first time that:

● **Sleeping Beauty was only asleep for 100 years because she had taken a massive dose of paracetamol**
● **Prince Charming was cold and indifferent to**

his lovely bride, and frequently rode off into the forest to visit his close friend Camilla Parker-Rapunzel
● **The Queen ruthlessly ignored the Princess's cries for help and continued to eat bread and honey in a callous manner**
● **In her distress Sleeping Beauty "binged" on pies stuffed with up to 24 blackbirds at a time**
● **The Princess's ugly sisters-in-law Fergiana and Anne, were allowed to get divorced but she wasn't.**

Close friends of Sleeping Beauty contacted by the Funday Times have confirmed that the story published last week by the Funday Times was totally accurate in every particular.

Grimm Stuff

Said one, who used to share a pumpkin with the Princess, "She used to be a fun-loving girl, who enjoyed balls and wearing glass slippers. But now she sits sadly in her turret, spinning a yarn which only the Funday Times is stupid enough to print in full".

CHARLES DROUGHT SPEECH

Everything's drying up

Not you, darling

"Harold? Oh, he's in the garden…"

IS IT THE END OF OUR BELOVED PRESS?

by Our Press Watching Staff

ONE of Britain's best-loved institutions is in crisis? Can the Royal press survive, after yet more revelations about the chaotic private lives of many of its senior members?

As he enters his 79th year, His Majesty the Digger seems to have lost all control over his younger employees, as they career from one scandal to another, leaving a train of marital disasters in their wake.

The Buck House Stops Here

There was a time when Royal watchers — men like Richard Dimbleby, Godfrey Winn and Kenneth Rose — were looked up to by the public, and carried out their duties conscientiously, untainted by scandal (except in the case of Godfrey Winn).

But today, as our picture-probe reveals, it is a different story.

Nigel Prince Dumpster. Balding, middle-aged, increasingly without a meaningful role, many observers wonder whether Prince-Dumpster will ever succeed in anything.

His marriage to the much younger aristocrat Lady Camilla has become a hollow sham. "They are never seen together in public," says a friend, "and they do not even share the same house."

Friends of Lady Camilla describe Dumpster as "vain, obsessed with publicising his cranky views in the media, cold, fish-like and utterly repulsive in every way."

Prince Andrew Neill. Balding, middle-aged, totally without a meaningful role, many observers are puzzled by the

fact that, at the age of 46, Prince Neill is still unmarried. Although his name has been linked with many young women, such as call-girl Pamella Bordes, none of his liaisons seem to last. Friends are worried that the public will soon draw "the obvious conclusion".

Lord Rothermere. Fat, balding, and without a meaningful role, many observers wonder what the 86-year-old Lord Rothermere is for. His marriage to the boisterous, fun-loving "Bubbles" has long been a hollow sham, as she shamelessly befriends visiting Texan millionaires and indeed almost anyone else.

Princess Antonia Holden. One time Keeper of the Royal Unauthorised Biographies, the balding, middle-aged

Holden has become an increasingly isolated figure, with no meaningful role.

As the first Royal biographer to have a much-publicised divorce, friends are worried that Princess Antonia spends all her time playing poker and writing mad letters to the *Times*, complaining that she is being persecuted by the Prince of Wales.

Let's Pargliamo Italiano

by Kilometra Kingtoni

No. 94: Meeting the Pope
Benvenuto al Vaticano!

POPE: I am Il Papa. Who are you?

ARCHBISHOP CAREY: Bongiorno. Dove Il Papa, per favore?

POPE: Sono Il Papa, idioto.

ARCHBISHOP CAREY: Scusi. Eco multi salutari di Chiesa Anglicari.

POPE: Grazia. Arrividerci. Have a nice giorno!

CAREY: Uno cappuccino, per favore.

POPE: Dominus vobiscum.

CAREY: I beg your pardon? Now about these women priests...

(Exit Pope)

© The Gnomophone Parliama Italiano – The Easy Way Cassette Course.

A Doctor writes

■ As a doctor I have often been asked in the last two weeks "why do I feel so sick, doctor?". The short answer is that you are almost certainly a victim of Bullshitia Murdocha, or "reading the papers", as it is more commonly known.

What happens is that the patient goes on a wild, compulsive binge, devouring huge quantities of junk and drivel about the Royal Family. After consuming several hundred columns of newsprint in a few hours, the patient then suddenly feels nausea, embarrassment and shame. In many cases they then throw up.

If you think you are suffering from bullshitia murdocha you should contact Andrew Neil immediately and be sick all over him.
© A Doctor.

"Quick, drive me into an early grave"

THE NEILL DIARIES

Private Eye has acquired for an unprecedented sum the secret diaries of one of the most hated men of the twentieth century. He was Andrew Neill, chief propagandist to the dictator Adolf Murdoch, who planned to take over the world.

THESE diaries have been examined by a team of experts, including Professor Hugh Very-Ropey and Professor Norman Stoned-Again, all of whom agree that the diaries are 100 per cent genuine in return for their usual cheques.

The Neill Diaries cover a crucial period in modern history when Murdoch was thought to be planning the elimination of the Royal Family as part of his masterplan. Written in a crude, barely legible Scottish scrawl, the Neill Diaries prove beyond a shadow of a doubt that Murdoch knew and approved of Neill's historic attack on the monarchy on what came to be known as Bullshitnacht.

"Bloody mature students"

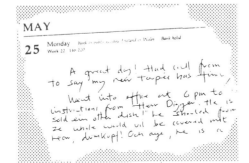

How the Diaries look

25th May

A great day! Had call from Brillowigs of St James's to say my new toupée has finally arrived.

Went into office at 6pm to receive my daily instructions from Herr Digger. He is very excited. "Ve haff sold ein other dish!" he shouted from his bunker. "Vun day ze whole world vill be covered mit dishes. All mine, do you hear, dumkopf!" Och aye, he is a wonderful man, the noo!

26th May

My new Armani suit is ready to pick up. I shall wear it to the opening of the new nightclub, Hooker's. I will be the talk of the town! At 6pm the phone rings. Always prompt, it is mein beloved Digger! As always he has fresh triumphs to report. "Mein latest blitzkrieg has destroyed ze BBC at a stroke," he told me. "Ve haff exclusive rights to all ze top football — here ve go, here ve go, here ve go! You must broadcast ze news in all mein papers. Is zat clear, schweinhund?" Oh how I worship this man!

Then he lets me in on the biggest secret of them all — the latest scheme in his masterplan to take over the world. We are going to eliminate the Royal Family!

3rd June

Der Digger's latest offensive against the hated Royals is going according to plan. How I hate them, these decadent parasites who are sapping the lifeblood of our beloved Fatherland, with their ridiculous palaces and fancy-dress rituals. But now, thanks to the Digger, we have a secret weapon that is going to blast them all into smithereens. It is code-named DIANA — HER OWN STORY. What a genius our leader is!

20th June

"Ze Royal Family is finished! Kaput!" So screamed mein glorious proprietor, Herr Murdoch, today when he rang me for my daily briefing. Together we laughed and toasted the downfall of the Old Britain and the triumph of Times International Socialism! The snobocracy is brought to its knees — Prince Charles, the snivelling Perry Worsthorne, and all the other toffs who sneer at me for my lowly upbringing, my bluff, down-to-earth manner, my Goebbels accent (*shurely 'Gorbals'? David Irving*), and my humble hairpiece (*shurely 'Herr-piece'? D.I.*).

© *World Copyright Irving Fasc-Trash Productions 1992*

JENNI MURRAY SPEAKS OUT

Hello. This is Woman's Whore

COMING SOON

EL DISASTERO –

the £200 million soap to end them all.

FOR YEARS thousands of craftsmen have been working round the clock to build a huge "working village" in the heart of London's Shepherds Bush.

Its purpose — to serve as the set for the most ambitious soap opera in history.

Forget *Neighbours, Dallas, EastEnders, The Late Show* — from this autumn the nation will be swept with *El Disastero* mania.

Last week the press were shown the lavish sets for the new soap, and introduced to the leading cast members of its fabulous cast who will become the household names of tomorrow:

His friend **"Johnny" Birt**, a chancer who has somehow drifted into El Disastero and ended up as the community's Mr Big.

Sex interest centres on the antics of "young", leggy, 57-year-old Cockney starlet **Janet Street-Porter**, who scandalises the community with her unending stream of young lovers and terrible programmes.

"Granny Esther", the local busybody who sticks her nose into everybody's business. Her catchphrase "That's Life" will soon be on the nation's lips.

"Mike" Checkland, the down-on-his-luck accountant who used to be a high flier, but now shuffles around waiting for the day when he will retire. Soon to be written out of the script.

(That's enough El Disastero. Ed.)

"Dukey" Hussey, the white-haired old disabled war veteran, who has retired to El Disastero to spend his declining years cocking up the BBC.

Al Yentob (real name "Botney"), the trendy, bearded layabout who dreams of being an "artist" — but all his efforts are doomed to failure.

And there's more sex too with sultry **Sarah Dunant** and her raunchy specs. She likes to hang about late at night chatting up weirdos when she thinks no one's watching (which they aren't).

GARRICK TO REMAIN BORES ONLY

by Our Clubland Staff **Quentin Lettsmakeupastory**

MEMBERS of the Garrick Club yesterday voted overwhelmingly by 396 to 0 to continue the Club's 178-year-old tradition as an all-bore preserve.

This spells the end for a recent campaign to allow non-bores into the club for the first time. Said a jubilant Sir Kingsley Bore, 85, who led the traditionalist opposition to the scheme: "This club was founded as a place where bores could meet each other and bore each other to death, if they felt like it. I am delighted that my fellow-members have been sensible enough to keep it that way."

Z-z-z-z

The well-known actor "Sir" Donald Bore was another who welcomed the landslide "no" vote. "It is not that we are against interesting people. It's just that we don't want to meet them here for lunch."

Sir Peregrine Boresthorne then woke up from his corner chair to point out in his typically controversial way that non-bores were already allowed in once a month, on the Non-Bore Guest Night, when the small dining room is made available for half an hour.

"With all the changes that have taken place in the modern world," said the silver-haired old crasher, "it is reassuring to know that there is one place left where you can be absolutely certain that you will meet nobody but a bore."

How they voted

Against: Sir Robin Bore, Mr Alan Watbores, Mr Geoffrey Wheatbore, Sir Louis Bore-Cooper QC, John Bortimer QC, Mr Melvyn Bore, Mr Giles Bordon (*That's enough bores, Ed.*)

"Run for it — it's the pratt and the fiddle"

THAT KELVIN MACKENZIE–TORY CENTRAL OFFICE PHONE CALL IN FULL

This is the complete and shocking transcript of the telephone conversation between a senior-ranking Tory Minister and the Editor of the *Sun*, Mr Kelvin Mackenzie OBE. It was obtained legally by bugging the *Sun*'s office with the help of trained burglars who were paid huge amounts of money by Lord Gnome.

Tapes (Ringing noise)
Sharon Tracy: Hello?
Mr X: Is that Mr MacFilth?
Tracy: Who wants him?
Mr X: Just say it's Mr X from Central Office.
Tracy: Kelvin, it's that Mr Wakeham again.
Mr X: No it isn't. It's the other one.
Tracy: Putting you through, Mr Baker.
Mr X: No, it's the other one.
Tracy: So sorry, Mr Patten.
Mr X: No…

Tracy: You're through now.
MacFilth: Who is it? I'm busy filling in me expenses.
Mr X: I have some rather interesting information for you, Mr MacFilth, concerning Mr Ashdown.
MacFilth: Who?
Mr X: The leader of the Liberal Party.
MacFilth: He's a poof is he? They usually are.
Mr X: No, he's quite the opposite. He's a bit of a ladies' man.
MacFilth: What? Legover? Now you're talking! I can see the Front Page already! Paddy Pantsdown! Vote Conservative!
Mr X: Yes, that's the sort of thing. John would be very pleased and there might be something in it for you.
MacFilth: A knighthood! Bugger me! The missus would like that. Go for it, squire. Just give me the names and addresses.
Mr X: Well actually we haven't got those as yet. We thought you chaps could just make them all up like you usually do.
MacFilth: What are you suggesting? That the *Sun* would tell whoppers? The only whoppers we've got is on page 3! Ha Ha Ha Ha! It's true, isn't it, Sharon?
Sharon (*listening on extension*): Yes, Mr MacFilth.
Mr X: Well, perhaps you could have a word with MI5. They've usually got some stuff on the opposition…
MacFilth: Nah, sorry Mr X. I'll have to pass on this one. You want to try the *Sunday Times*, it's more their sort of thing. If you hang on, Sharon will put you through.
(*Short burst of "Eine Kleine Nachtmusik"*)
Scottish voice: Hello there, have you got any filth?
Mr X: I've something rather good on Paddy Ashdown.
Andrew Neill (*for it is he*): Is he a poof then?
(*Tape ends*)

BATTYWOMAN RETURNS

TROUBLE starts when Battywoman, whom everyone thought had been killed off in the last film, is found miraculously preserved in the House of Lords. The sexy Lady is soon brandishing her whip and terrorising her old enemy, Greyman. Not suitable for children.

Now showing at the following Gnomeons

Hailsham **Archole** **Tebbit Park**
Baker Street **Ridley North** **Parkinson**

David Mellor. Gap-toothed, mop-headed Minister for Fuck *(shurely 'Fun'? Ed)*.

MELLOR DRAMA

Who are they — the key players in the Scandal of the Century? **The Private Eye Guide** that clears up the confusion.

Professor Keays. Outraged father-in-law of David Steel's home-loving wife Judy who compared actress Sarah de Keays to cartoon character Olive Oyl and said of son-in-law Parkinson: "David is an awfully nice chap who should be strung up. It's the only language he understands." *(Shurely sheveral mishtakes? Ed.)*

Pamella de Sancha. Sultry Indian actress who bewitched the Minister by sucking up to the Tories *(shurely 'toes'? Ed)*.

Paul Melloran. Mystery journalist and friend of top Tory David English *(shurely 'Mellor'? Ed)*.

Dominic Pratt. Mystery journalist and former lover of Christina de Keela. No one knows why he has a job *(shurely shome mishtake? Ed)*.

MAJOR BACKS PRIVACY BILL IN WAKE OF SCANDAL

by our Political Staff
Dominic Pratt

THE Prime Minister has given his personal backing to a "draconian new Bill" to curb the power of the press in revealing matters that are "of no public interest".

He has let it be known that he is furious at the way the recent Government scandal has been plastered all over newspaper front pages.

Sources close to John Major say that he feels the press has gone too far this time and that it can no longer be relied upon to act responsibly.

Cock-up

Said one senior figure: "John does not expect to see the private details of Britain's economic problems splashed all over the tabloids. Nor does he want to read accounts of Norman Lamont's financial performance over his breakfast. Politicians are entitled to a degree of privacy over their professional lives. Of course they are not saints and there are limits to what the public can reasonably expect from their elected representatives in terms of their personal competence."

The source continued: "Norman Lamont has been put through hell by the press just because he made a few mistakes with the economy. This is nobody's business but his own and the needless suffering that he and loved ones like John Major have gone through is disgraceful."

The Prime Minister will be introducing the new Bill as a first measure in clamping down on press intrusion into political life."

ON OTHER PAGES

"Recession over" says Lamont   p.3
"Leg over" says Mellor   p.6

THE BIG MATCH

Has anyone scored, David?

Yes, me...

Desert Island Dics

(shurely 'Discs'? Ed)

Your cut-out-'n'-keep souvenir guide to the Minister of Fun's historic selection of eight records

1. Sibelius *Legovia Suite In A Friend's Flat.*
The Battersea Symphony Orchestra. Solo Buffoon: P. Halloran.

2. Bach's *Tocata and Fuck* (*shurely 'Fugue'? Ed*) for solo organ (D. Mellor).

3. Love Duet from Donizetti's *I Adulterati* (sung by Kiri Tee Hee Hee and Dietrich Compact-Dieskau).

4. Schubert's *Die Schöne Mellorin*
Robert Endintears (tenor). Gerald Moretocome (piano).

5. Gabriel Foureye's *Requiem in J Major*
Conservative Central Office Choir conducted by Sir Norman Fowler.

6. Bach's *Air on a G-String* (arranged for the Mellors Ensemble by Paolo Hallorani).

7. Debussy's *Après-Midi d'Un Fornicator*
Orchestre de Lettres Francais. Conducted by Sir Branson Mates.

8. Purcell's *Strumpet Voluntary*
Antonia de Sancha (strumpet). D. Mellor (horn).

Luxury: Take-Away Pizza.

THE SUN

HOW THE PAKIS CHEATED

by Mickey Mouse, England's Team Manager

YES! The Pakis cheated. That was the only explanation for England's shock defeat in the last Test.

As England team manager, I was in a unique position to see for myself the disgraceful below-the-belt tactics employed by the Pakistani bowlers, Wassim Howzat, Wakki Yurout and Yosser Mustache *(Who they? Ed)*.

I can reveal the Pakis deliberately bowled:

● **Really fast**
● **At the stumps**
● **Spinning it as well.**

The result was that the batsman could not see the ball, let alone hit it, and was thus put in an impossible position. I say these cheats should be strung up and sent home.

© M. Mouse, SunTrash.

TEST MATCH SCORE IN FULL

1st Innings

Pakistan   798-0 declared
(Mianmigirl 700 n.o.)

England   13 All Out
(Yosser 10 for 1)

2nd Innings

England   0 All Out
(Yurout 10 for 0)

Pakistan won by Innings and 785 runs

APOLOGY
from Mr N. Lamont and others

Over the past 13 years, this Government may have given the impression that it was considered desirable for members of the public to save their money. Such savings may have been considered to be the basis for investment in Britain's economic future. It was on this understanding that the Conservative Government may have given the impression that it supported wider share ownership and a policy of wholesale privatisation, so that Britain could leap forward into an age of prosperity unparalleled in the history of the world.

We now recognise and fully accept that the greatest obstacle to any economic recovery is the quite disgraceful habit of "saving". Don't people realise that it is their pathetic reluctance to "spend, spend, spend" and if necessary borrow vast sums of money in order to buy new videos and K-registration Ford Sierras which is rapidly driving this country into a state of bankruptcy, with millions unemployed and no end to the recession in sight?

We would like to express our regret for any confusion which our previous statements may inadvertently have caused, and offer our profound and sincere apologies for the total chaos that the country is now in, which is entirely the fault of the general public for being a bunch of penny-pinching misers.

© N. Lamont, Villa Chancellori, Tuscany

MEDUSA HITS PUBERTY

KINDRED SPIRITS *Custard lovers*

Lord Tonypandy
"I grew up in Wales. Times were hard and in the Valleys if you had custard you were one of the nobs. I can remember the first time I ever tasted real custard was in a Lyon's Corner House near the House of Commons."

Sir Yehudi Menuhin
"Whenever I am abroad playing Brahms and Schumann, I always think of England — the green fields, the leafy lanes and your wonderful bowls of delightful custard. American custard does not taste as fine — one of the reasons why I decided to settle on these shores."

Frank Bruno
"I always eat a bowl of custard before a big fight. My manager says it does me good and helps me to relax."

Alan Bennett
"When I was a little boy we'd all go round on Saturday nights to Aunt Abigail's for custard butties, which she made specially for us little ones. Then one day she got taken poorly in the supermarket. It was kidney failure, the doctors said. After the funeral we *(contd p. 94)*

Michael Fish
"Custard looks like falling in many parts of Scotland and Northern Ireland — moving across Central England by mid-day, it could be thick in places. So, if you're taking the car out, mind how you go."

Lady Diana Mosley
"I never liked custard as a little gel. I remember Charity and I being force-fed the stuff by Nanny Soames in the nursery at Waldegrave. When we visited the Führer at Berchtesgarten we were served the most delicious German 'Black Custard'. Hitler made it himself on a little Bavarian log-stove. I can see him now…"

It's not cricket

by Imran Khantwrite

THERE was absolutely no excuse whatsoever for the Pakistani players shouting abuse at the umpire during the third Test Match. The umpire's decision is always final, and players should treat him with respect at all times. If our captain Javed Miandad had any grievance, he should have raised it privately after play was over.

But, frankly, umpire Palmer's behaviour was quite disgraceful to my mind. Did you see the way he handed back that sweater to poor Aqib Javed, without even a smile or a friendly pat on the shoulder?

I mean, all that Aqib had done was bowl a few bouncers when Palmer had asked him not to. And, anyway, if the English batsmen haven't got the bottle to stand there while our lads chuck it down at them, then they are just a lot of lily-livered little white poofs, like Devon Malcolm, and they should take up another sport like croquet.

As for the racist umpire Palmer, he should be strung up. It is the only language people like him understand.

© *Tariq Ali. Cab No. 505-9 (dec).*

A Doctor writes

As a doctor I am often asked, "Doctor, have you got Aids?"

The short answer is "Mind your own business." If you're worried that your doctor might have Aids, bad luck.

© *A. Doctor (decd.)*

"One day, son, all this will be theirs"

MIKE TURNER

BBC2

A season of Woody Allen films to commemorate the celebrated director's affair with his wife's daughter.

Introduced by Alex Cock *(shurely 'Cox'? Ed).*

Custody shock

Of course she is an unfit mother – she had an affair with Woody Allen

Friday 10.00 pm

Mia and Her Daughters

BLACK and white classic in which Allen plays a neurotic Jewish New York film director who runs off with the adopted daughter of his wife from an earlier marriage. Also stars Mia Farrow and Soon-Yi Previn.

Saturday 9.30 pm

Madhatter

ALLEN at his most endearing, paying tribute to himself in this wry Jewish New York look at a neurotic film director who falls in love with a 21-year-old girl whom he meets in his wife's apartment. Includes the unforgettable comic scene when his wife discovers nude pictures of her daughter. Stars Mia Farrow, Allen himself and hundreds of lawyers .

Sunday 11.30 pm

Do It Again, Woody

PLAYFUL parody of *Casablanca* in which a neurotic middle-aged Jewish film-maker goes to a bar in New York and falls in love with his wife's daughter. Glorious mixture of tears and laughter. Don't miss the embarrassing bedroom scene. Stars Mia Farrow and Woody Woodpecker.

Sunday 1.30 am

Bananas

MIDDLE-aged neurotic Jewish film maker goes bananas and runs off with his wife's daughter, then thinks he'll get custody of their children. "He's really bananas," says his mother-in-law, played by Maureen O'Sullivan in a typical one-liner. Also stars Andre Previn, Frank Sinatra, Diane Keaton, Michael Caine and Woody from *Cheers*.

(That's enough films. Ed.)

How they are related

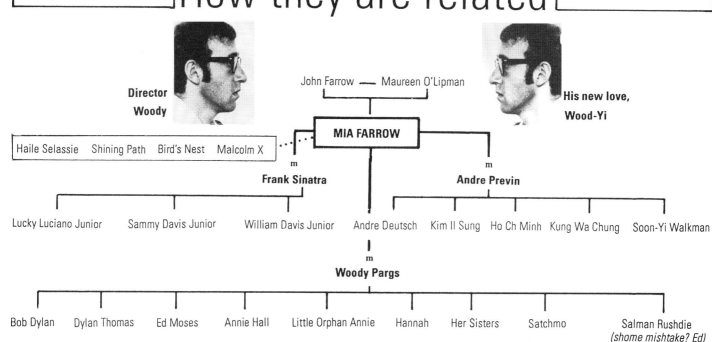

Director Woody

John Farrow —— Maureen O'Lipman

His new love, Wood-Yi

| Haile Selassie | Shining Path | Bird's Nest | Malcolm X |

MIA FARROW

m — **Frank Sinatra**

m — **Andre Previn**

Lucky Luciano Junior — Sammy Davis Junior — William Davis Junior — Andre Deutsch — Kim Il Sung — Ho Ch Minh — Kung Wa Chung — Soon-Yi Walkman

m — **Woody Pargs**

Bob Dylan — Dylan Thomas — Ed Moses — Annie Hall — Little Orphan Annie — Hannah — Her Sisters — Satchmo — Salman Rushdie

(shome mishtake? Ed)

MELLOR TAKES 'TEA' WITH PLO SEX BOMB

Parliament to be recalled

by Our Court Staff P.L. O'Booze

TOP QC Mr George Carphone today accused Fun Minister David Mellor of "entirely innocent love romps" over a "cup of tea" with a wealthy blonde who has close links with people who have close links with other people who have seen international terrorist Saddam Hussein being interviewed on television.

Cross-examining Mrs Mona Lisa, 32, the legendary forensic interrogator showed no mercy.

CARPHONE: While I am in no way suggesting that a "cup of tea" in this context represents anything more than a totally innocent act of intercourse between consenting adults *(Court laughs at legendary wit)*, was it nevertheless not inviting misinterpretation for you, an attractive young woman, to be alone for up to 20 minutes with a well-known political lothario and his wife?

MRS BOWWOW: I resent that suggestion. The Palestinian Liberation Organisation is a humanitarian organisation, entirely devoted to helping elderly, disabled Americans off the decks of cruise liners.

CARPERSON: That is all very well, is it not? But I would ask the court to look at these photographs. *(Intake of breath from jury and cries of "Great, here comes the dirty bit")* Would you, or would you not agree, Mrs Arafat, that this is a picture of yourself in a skimpy three-piece bathing suit?

SIR HARTLEY REDFACE QC *(for Mrs Gadaffi):* I object, Your Honour. I fail to see where this line of questioning is taking us.

MR JUSTICE COCKLE-DRAKE: I am finding it increasingly interesting. Pray continue, Sir George — and could the usher please arrange for copies of those photographs to be placed in my private chamber?

CARDRIVER: Mrs Hussein, were we to imagine you removing this suit, would we not find you wearing items of underclothing — perhaps skimpy, perhaps lacy?

JUDGE: Who are Messrs Skimpy and Lacy?

REDFACE: I believe, My Lord, that they are female detectives in a televisual entertainment set in the United States of America.

MRS BAUHAUS: I resent that imputation. Mr Mellor and I only met on two occasions, to discuss classical music and the prospects for a settlement of the Gaza Strip problem.

CARBOOT: Was Mr Mellor wearing the Gazza Strip when you made love — or, rather, enjoyed a cup of tea?

(Court erupts in paroxysms of hysteria as hacks note down latest bon mot of Gray's Inn's Mr Filth)

Earlier the court had heard the editor of the *Sunday Mellor*, Mr Richard Snott, describe his story headed DAVE'S AT IT AGAIN as "in the highest traditions of investigative journalism".

MR REDFACE: Do you recall, do you not, the precise circumstances in which your article was printed, was it not?

SNOTT: Yeah, I do, so help me God. Our boys were about to go in to the Gulf. The lives of British lads was on the line. It was a moment of supreme national crisis. And what was the so-called Minister for Football doing? He was sitting there having a cosy cuppa with some Arab bint. Makes you sick, dunnit?

JUDGE: I am sorry, Mr Stoat. Are you suggesting that in some way it was the tea which made you feel indisposed? But, talking of tea, I see it is now half-past two and we have been back from lunch for more than five minutes. Perhaps this would be a good time for the Court to adjourn until tomorrow morning, as I have a number of important photographs to examine.

The Court adjourned.

A Doctor writes

AS a doctor I am often asked "Doctor, should Ludovic Kennedy be put to sleep?" The simple answer is yes.

What happens is that a number of people feel increasing pain at the sight of this elderly broadcaster endlessly repeating his arguments about euthanasia or, to give it the full medical name, *Ludovica arenchasicofimensis*.

Often, after exposure to Ludovic Kennedy, the patient falls asleep into a state of terminal boredom from which there is no recovery.

If you are worried about Ludovic Kennedy, you should avoid all contact with newspapers and television.

©*A. Doctor*

New storm over embarrassing Royal pictures

by **ANDREW MORTONSOFGARBAGE**
Royal Staff

THE beleaguered Royal Family faced fresh controversy today with the discovery of a series of embarrassing pictures by Prince Charles.

The controversial watercolours were found in a remainder shop in a pile of unsold books entitled "All One's Own Work".

Outrage

The portraits, some showing graphic scenes of Scottish landscapes, are believed to have been taken by very few bookshops and have netted the publishers very little money at all.

Shame

The Palace denied that the pictures were scandalous. "They're not that bad," said one spokesman. "The one of the little farmhouse in Tuscany is OK, isn't it?"

Shock

But hardened Royal watchers are more cynical. "The Royal Family are really in trouble now. The shame of it will be unbearable. A Royal coffee-table book that doesn't sell any copies — it's the end of Royalties as they know them."

FERGIE — AMAZING NEW PICTURES

The incredible pictures on pp 1, 2, 3, 4, 5, 6, 7 and 94 of this issue show the Duchess of York as you have never seen her before.

These unbelievable photographs are entirely unique. They show the Duchess fully clothed and not on holiday.

You won't believe your eyes. Yet these pics, taken by world-famous *Eye* lensman Gino Ginelli from an XF-36 satellite orbiting 80 miles above the Duchess, are completely authentic.

Many people may criticise us for publishing these shocking photographs. They may say that what the Duchess does during her Royal life is entirely her own affair.

But we say that we all have a right to know the real truth behind the Duchess of York's carefully contrived public image as a lazy, fat slag who is sponging off the taxpayer.

Hard at work

Wearing clothes

With her husband

That Fergie Poolside Lunch Menu in full

Tomatoe Salad or Toeramasalata

— ❋ —

Feetucine Toescana

— ❋ —

Toed in the Hole
with
Duchess of Yorkshire Pudding, Boiled Potatoes and Haritoes Verts

— ❋ —

Profitoerolles

— ❋ —

Cheese on Toes

— ❋ —

Wines
Chatoe Lafeet 1992
or
Toejolais Nouveau Riche

— ❋ —

Toe or Coffee

Those Kuwaiti Elections in full

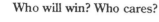

Kuwait (Central)
No change
100% Turnout (All 3 people voted)
His Royal Highness Prince Box-

wallah al-Sabbatical (Emir al-Sabbatical's Royalist Democratic Fascist Dictatorship United Alliance For a Palestinian-Free Kuwait)   3 votes

Masif al-Bedoon (Opposition Party)   0 votes.

Mr Bedoon has sadly disappeared. Obituary — page 94.

BEGINNING TODAY

THE LAWSON MEMOIRS

The man described by himself as "The Most Brilliant Chancellor Ever" looks back at his years in office and describes just how brilliant he was.

Part One: I was Terrifically Brilliant

I shall never forget the day when I told Mrs Thatcher just how brilliant I was. It was in a cabinet meeting and she turned to me and said "I think we should give in to Arthur Scargill." This was typical of her "give-in" approach to everything: the Unions, Europe and the Argentinians.

Fortunately for her, I was there to give her some backbone and come up with the brilliant ideas needed to save the country.

TOMORROW: How I could easily have been Prime Minister but I couldn't be bothered.

Lawson's Sensational Verdicts

Mrs Thatcher: *"Weak, vacillating, not as good as me."*

Norman Tebbit: *"Shy, weak, ineffectual. Not as good as me."*

Geoffrey Howe: *"Tough, decisive, combative. But still not as good as me."*

Bernard Ingham: *"Bastard."*

Government to close down country

56 billion jobs to go

By **JOHN COLEFACE**
Ex-Political Editor

THE PRIME Minister last night announced the most wide-ranging shakeout in Britain's history.

As from this Friday, the entire country is to be closed down.

"I deeply regret that we have had to make this move," Mr Major explained, "but the country is no longer economically viable.

"However," he went on, "I am glad to say that we have been able to arrange extremely generous compensation for all those affected, amounting to £1 billion for every man, woman and child in the country."

Giving further details of the Government's shock "rationalisation" programme, Mr Heseltine went on to warn that the Government itself might have to be closed down if things carried on as they have done.

Mineless Vandalism

"I blame the world recession," he told no one at all, "not to mention the Bundesbank, Lady Thatcher, Arthur Scargill and everyone who voted Conservative at the last election.

"If they hadn't voted Tory on 9 April," he screamed, "we wouldn't be in the mess we're in today."

'PEACE IN OUR TIME'

Nation Rejoices as British Prime Minister Returns from Germany

A TIRED but triumphant Mr John Majorlain stepped off the plane today after his historic talks with the German Chancellor, Herr Kohl.

Holding aloft a ten-pound note, he declared, "I have in my hand a piece of paper. And it's completely worthless."

A-Ten-Pees-ment

Mr Neville Major continued:

"There will be no war of words with Germany. I have spoken to Herr Kohl, who has promised me that the Bundesbank will not invade any other currencies until they feel like it."

Waiting crowds at the airport jeered wildly as Mr Majorlain pledged a new era of cooperation. "Herr Kohler will do what he likes and we will cooperate." The pound is 2.173 DM.

GERMAN V-SIGN CELEBRATIONS NOT TO GO AHEAD

by Our Euro-Staff **Robert "Bomber" Harris**

A STORM of outrage in all parts of Britain has greeted the news that the German government is to erect a massive 3,000-foot high "V-sign" to commemorate the destruction of the Pound.

It is now almost exactly two weeks since the much-vaunted Pound Sterling came under a blitzkrieg assault from the massed armadas of the dreaded Bundesbanktodtsbattalienen.

All Quiet On The NatWest Front

Said one British veteran of those dramatic few hours in the autumn of 1992:

"How could those beastly Germans be so insensitive to the feelings of those of us who lost everything during the Battle of the Pound? Thousands of jobs were wiped out in the course of a single afternoon, as those Boche bankers launched their dreaded V-Sign at London. We were quite defenceless. We surrendered immediately."

But from Germany last night, where the champagne was still flowing in the streets, one jubilant bomber shouted out: "Today England, tomorrow the World Bank."

*"Oh, Doctor — how **awful** to be expected to diagnose symptoms at a dinner party!"*

NICK DOWNES

KINDRED SPIRITS
People who should resign

Sir Robin Leigh-Pemberton

"I should resign," says the Bank of England governor. "The BCCI scandal was ultimately my fault but I don't see why I should take the blame."

Marmaduke Hussey
"There is an incontrovertible argument for my resignation," says the Chairman of the BBC. "It's nothing to do with my age — I'm just not up to it. But I've no intention of going."

Norman Lamont

"People have said for months that I should resign." So says the Chancellor of the Exchequer, but he is adamant that he will not step down. "Since when did total incompetence disqualify a man from holding down a top job?"

Michael Heseltine
The President of the Board of Trade has no doubts about his position. "Take it from me," he said. "I'm not moving from here. No matter how many cock-ups I make, I'm staying. It's a matter of principle."

Graham Taylor
The England soccer manager doesn't mince his words. "I see this as a job for life. Just because we lose every time is no reason to blame me. I only pick the team."

John Major
"I'm definitely not going to resign," says the decisive Prime Minister of Great Britain. "Or maybe I am. I'm not sure. It's not my fault the country's in a mess. Which it isn't. Or is it?"

"Well, it's not a cultural desert – that's Michael Ignatieff and Waldemar Januszcak"

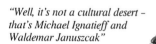

HOUSE OF WINDSOR SAFARI PARK TO CLOSE

by Our Conservation Staff **Zoo Lawley**

ONE of the country's best-loved amusements is scheduled to close due to lack of public support, it was revealed yesterday.

At its peak the House of Windsor attracted millions of enthusiastic lovers of wildlife, many of whom came from all over the world to catch a glimpse of the rare species on display.

Sadly, as a result of the recession and a general public reaction against the keeping of exotic creatures at taxpayers' expense, the enterprise is now on the verge of collapse.

Save the Wales

The principal concern is the fate of the creatures in the likely event of closure.

A spokesman for the Park said: "They cannot fend for themselves and there is no demand for them elsewhere. In the old days everyone wanted to see a Queen or a Prince or even a Duchess, but nowadays no one is interested.

"The humane option would be to put them all to sleep," he continued, "but the sentimentalists would be up in arms."

FACT FILE
THE FERGIE

● It costs £8 billion a year just to feed one Fergie.

● Fergies cannot survive the English winter and have to be sent abroad to hot climates.

● The Fergie needs to mate frequently with different partners. Limited success has been achieved recently with a Texan breed.

TOMORROW: The Chazza — why it goes mad in captivity.

Emergency services failed Humpty

by Our Nursery Rhyme Staff **Polly Toynbeeputthekettleon**

MR HUMPTY Dumpty was left lying at the bottom of a wall for several hours yesterday before emergency services arrived at the scene.

All the King's Horses and All the King's Men took three and a half hours to reach the accident after being alerted by neighbours.

Said an old woman who lived in a shoe: "Mr Dumpty was just sitting on the wall and then he had a great fall. I dialled the King's Men at once but nothing happened. The delay must have seriously impaired Mr Dumpty's chances of being put together again."

The Head of All the King's Horses and All the King's Men has offered his resignation after explaining that the computer system had sent his men to the wrong wall, where they had merely found ten green bottles. "By then," he admitted, "the standard 14½ minutes had elapsed and by the time we got to Mr Dumpty he was unfortunately scrambled."

Elsewhere two children, one of whom had a broken crown, were forced to wait at the bottom of a hill for most of a day. Jack, 4, and Jill, 3 (whose surnames have been omitted to protect their identity) were last night said to be "improving". Their mother, however, was furious, claiming: "If it hadn't been for the prompt action of Dr Foster, who happened to be passing on his way to Gloucester, it could have been really serious."

Not so lucky was Little Jack Horner, who, after accidentally getting a plum stuck on his thumb, was taken to the casualty department at St Mary Mary (The Quite Contrary)'s Teaching Hospital.

He was told on arrival: "Oh no. This has been closed down by the Tomlinson report."

Old Mother Hubbard is 108.

THAT KINNOCK JY PROG IN FULL

What You Missed

Kinnock: Hullo and totally welcome to the utterly totally JY Prog. This is Neil Kinnock and I'm the former leader of the Labour Party and I'm totally and utterly and utterly and totally delighted to be both presenting, fronting and presenting from the Front later on I'll be playing some records and doing interviews but first I'll be playing records as I've said and I've made perfectly clear from the beginning of the programme and then I'll be doing interviews which I've also said all along so without further ado let's get on with looking ahead at what's in the programme and I would like to state categorically with total frankness and utter categorical stateness that the time has come for a change people are sick and tired of Jimmy Young people are crying out for someone who can get this programme moving again play records people want interview the sort of celebrities that the public actually like oh I could murder a curry *(continues until 1.00 News).*

HOW IT WILL WORK

By Penny JunoanythingabouttheRoyalscauseIdon't and James "Deeplysaddened" Whattakreep
(with no additional material by Nigel Pratt-Dumpster)

FOLLOWING the sensational break-up of the Royal Marriage announced last week, two very contrasting courts will wield the Royal Power into the next century, *writes Lady Antonia Wholly-Guesswork (author of "The Prince Charles I Never Met").*

These are the new look "separate courts" of Charles and Diana:

The Chazzites

1. Belinda Harpie, 37. Formidable, gorgeous, pouting PR expert who will advise the Prince on key issues such as choice of trousers.

2. Sir Laurens Van der Pump, 99. Long-time spiritual mentor to the Prince. Will advise on key issues such as auspicious dates in the calendar for travelling, money and romance.

3. Lady Legovia Amstrad-Barker, 45. Long-time confidante and intimate of the Prince. Will advise on key issues such as what to wear under his trousers.

4. Dr Jonathon Porridge, 43. Environmentalist and agrarian economist. Will advise Prince on key issues such as what cereal he should eat with his breakfast.

The Di-Hards

1. Lieutenant Archie Dingball-Twytte, 33. 27th/41st Queen's Own Hooray Henries. A long-time friend of the Princess, he will advise on key issues such as how terrific she looks in that pink dress.

2. Lady Georgie Cavendish, 31. Long-term schoolchum and flatmate of Diana's. She will advise on key issues such as how awful Charles is, how right she was to leave him, and how she should ring up the *Sun* and tell them all about it.

3. Mother Theresa of Calcutta, 92. Key admirer of Diana's charity work. Mother Teresa will advise the Princess on how to get into the same photograph as herself.

4. Giuseppe Calamari, 49. Patron of the fashionable Knightsbridge restaurant *San Wichbar*. He will advise on Today's Specials, such as spaghetti carbonara or spaghetti bolognese. He will also wield a giant pepper pot and say "Bella, bella, Principessa" in a sycophantic voice.

(That's enough courtiers. Ed.)

𝕿𝖍𝖊 𝕷𝖎𝖛𝖊𝖘 𝖔𝖋 𝖙𝖍𝖊 𝕾𝖆𝖎𝖓𝖙𝖘 𝕹𝖔. 94
THE BLESSED SELWYN OF GUMMER

LITTLE is known about St Selwyn, who lived in the Dark Ages. However, no one was a greater champion of the Church of England than St Selwyn and he frequently defended it against heresy. In 1992 AD the Synod voted to ordain women and St Selwyn decided to leave the Church altogether rather than tolerate this wickedness.

As a sign that he had made the right decision in the eyes of God, this holy man was blessed with what became known as the Miracle of the Pond.

This pond had hitherto been nothing more than a small dirty pool, full of rubbish and old tins, at the bottom of Selwyn's garden.

But one day it was suddenly transformed into a beautiful, clean, home-enhancing water complex with golden fish and exotic water lilies. And folk came from all Christendom to see for themselves the Holy Pond of Gummer.

The wicked murmured among themselves that it was a huge bribe from an agricultural corporation. But the faithful knew only too well that it was a symbol of divine grace operating through St Selwyn.

Ye Daily Tudorgraph

Edited by Ye Marquess of Haftings
at ye Canarie Wharf

Conradde ye Blakke. Prop.   2 Groats   15 December in Ye Yeare of Our Lorde 1529

ROYAL FPLIT SHOCKE
COUPLE TO LEAD FEPARATE LIVES

by our Correfpondent Master Hugh Montgomerie of Massingberdde

YE WHOLE nation was faddened by ye fenfational news that his Majesty King Henry and his Queen Katharine have decided to live feparately.

At present there are no plans for ye King to behead her.

Ye couple have "a deep refpect" for each other, and have reached an "amicable agreement" never to meet again.

ANDREW MORTON'S FORK

Ye King, 49 stone, plans to set up the new Church of England which will allow him to do whatever he likes.

Archbishop Carey faid today: "There if no reason why a power-crazed divorced lunatic should not be head of the Church of England, but quoth me not, old boy, or I might end up in ye fire."

Courtiers were quick to express fympathy for ye King and ye Queen in their "time of forrow and fadness". Said My Lord St John of Wolsley: "The hearts and prayers of all ye nation go out to the unhappy couple."

"And we muft hope," he added, "that from now on ye fcribblers and all manner of hackes will refpect ye privacy of ye King and ye Queene."

A recent ftudie of Ye King by Mafter Holbein

"NO THIRD PARTY INVOLVED IN FPLIT"

by TV's Sir Thomas More, Editor of Ye Lord's Daye Tudorgraph

A palace spokesman was quick to deny that any third parties were involved in the tragic Royal separation.

Recent reports had linked the name of His Gracious Majesty with Mistrefs Anne Boleyn, a pouting upper-class beauty. But this is difmissed as "pure fpeculation" by Mafter Carter Rucke, the Royal Libelmafter, who threatened that anyone who repeated these "grofs and wicked flanders" would be burned at the ftake.

FAIRY TALE ROMANCE THAT ENDED IN TEARS

Can it only have been in the year of Our Lorde 1502 that the handsome, dashing Prince Hal wedded ye beautiful Princess Katharine from Aragon?

Their nuptial celebrations in ye Abbey were witnessed by a record 350 people.

Yet today ye dream has turned to afhes (continued folio 94).

Miftress Glenda Slagge of Ye Streete By Ye Fleete River

Ye Wench They Cannot Gagge

Hats off to ye Royal Couple for their honestic and courage in facing up to ye problem suffered by one in 3 million married couples in Tudor England todaye.

I faye "Heads Off" to everyone — except of course Hif Majeftie!

Here they are — Miftress Glenda's Yummy Yeomen of 1529!!

Ye Duke of Somerfet — so he hath ye poxe, but who hathn't?

Ye Earl of Northumberland — ditto.

Sir Marmalade of Gusset — crazy name, crazy guy!

ON OTHER PAGES

The Alternative Rocky Horror Service Book

No. 94. The Blessing Of On-Going Same-Sex Relationships Between Meaningful Adults

The President *(Bishop Spong, for it is he or she):* Dearly and openly beloved brothers and sisters. We are gathered together here today to share the sacrament of safe sex between N— or N— (here he shall name the consenting adults who wish to be joined together in wholly ludicrous matrimony). Who giveth this condom unto this man?

N: I do.

President: Who receiveth this condom?

N: I do.

President: Then I must ask you both to say after me: "I hereby give you this condom as a symbol of my belief in safe sex, and my admiration for Elizabeth Taylor."

(There shall then be played a suitable piece of music, as it may be "Over The Rainbow" by Judy Garland, or "It's Raining Men" by the Weather Girls. If those to be joined together are of a female orientation, then the exchange of condoms shall be replaced by selected recitations from Ms Jeanette Winterson. It may be "Oranges Are Not The Only Fruit", or it may be some similar work. There shall then be a reading from the Gospel According To Spong)

"And it came to pass that he took unto himself twelve young men, none of whom were married. And they went about together, eating, drinking and going to parties. And he said unto them "If any man would leave his father and his mother and follow, then I shall show him a good time, for I know all the places.

And there were two women living in the same house, Mary and Martha, who were clearly, you know what. I mean it's obvious, isn't it?"

Here ends the reading.

The President shall then invite the congregation to join with him in the Kiss, or some such similar act of physical contact denoting the Sacrament of Same Sex Relationships. The congregation shall then sing something appropriate from *100 Hymns For The Gay*. **It may be No. 94, "Would You Like To Abide With Me?"**

NEXT WEEK: A Service of Consolation for the Break-up of a Same-Sex Relationship (including the division of the Shirley Bassey record collection, or it may be the motor cycle boots).

©SPCGay Publishing Co, with Foreword by the Bishop of Durham.

MATRIX-CHURCHILL — THREE FOUND NOT GUILTY

by our Cover-Up Staff
Lord Justice Scott-Free

Lucky not to be in prison

THREE Cabinet Ministers accused of attempting to pervert the course of justice were today acquitted by themselves following a two-second hearing in front of the Prime Minister.

The three men, pictured above, were charged with blatantly trying to suppress evidence, thereby bringing about the conviction of three innocent businessmen.

At the first and last minute, Mr Kenneth Clark, Mr Malcolm Rifkind and Mr Michael Tarzan were told that they had no case to answer.

"If we went down," said Mr Clark, "where would it all stop? Everyone was doing it. Garel-Jones, John Major, Mrs Thatcher. All of us. It was Government Policy at the time."

The men celebrated with champagne before being driven off to tell some more lies on television.

One of Britain's Greatest Living Writers, A.N. Wislon, retells

THE CHRISTMAS STORY

as it probably happened

JOSEPH and Mary probably never met. Recent research suggests that, if he existed, Joseph was not a carpenter but a rich nobleman, living in what is now Iraq. Historians have long known that the story of the census in the time of Augustus was made up in the 4th century by the Roman historian Nedus Sherrinus as an amusing after-dinner anecdote. Archaeologists have discovered no stables in the area around Bethlehem, so Jesus was most likely born at home in a tent (or possibly underwater in Lake Tiberius). The "shepherds", long familiar from the Gospel story, were in fact Palestinian terrorists out to overthrow the Roman administration. This confusion arose from the similarity of the Hebrew word "sephardim" (terrorists) and

the English word "shepherds".
A happy Christmas to you all.
© *Christopher Sincere-Stevenson 1992*

Is there a sale on at Threshers?

DIANA TO CHOOSE ST CAKE'S?

by Our Education Staff
G.C.S.E. Fail

THERE IS a strong possibility that the future heir to the throne is to be educated at the little-known public school St Cake's rather than the more traditional Eton.

A spokesman for the Princess Regent said yesterday that St Cake's had many advantages over other schools of its kind. "In particular," he said, "security would not pose a problem because no one knows where it is."

Rip-Off

St Cake's (motto: Who Pays Wins A Place) was founded in 1442 by King Henry VII and is the oldest school in the world, according to its brochure compiled by leading London PR firm Hogleby, Bowtie & Nogleby.

The new Headmaster, appointed only last week, is a former accountant, Mr Reginald Checkland, a cousin of the BBC Director-General, who is himself an Old Cakesian.

Other famous Old Boys of the school include Jeremy Paxman, Robin Leigh Pemberton and composer Johnny Dankworth.

Very High Fees

Prince Wills, if he were selected, could well end up in Parker-Bowles, the House named after the Rev. Norbert Parker-Bowles, founder of the school (1826-1872).

Said Housemaster of C Dorm, Mr Roy Terreblanche: "He will be very welcome here. The boys are all very stupid but we beat them into shape, ha ha ha."

Prince Wills is 2.

"Your usual table?"

PETER CARTER-RUCK AND PARTNERS

SOLICITORS
PRIVY COUNCIL AGENTS
INCORPORATING
CHRISTOPHER SMITH & CO

75 SHOE LANE
LONDON EC4A 3BQ

To Mr N. Lamont
c/o HM Treasury Accounts Dept.

TO: Receiving phone call from you on 6.7.92.

TO: My secretary advising you I was in a meeting and asking you if you wished to hold.

TO: Your listening to Handel's *Water Music* during lengthy waiting period.

TO: My eventually coming on the line and listening to your account of your difficulties in connection with your tenant Miss Whiplash.

TO: Removal of standard eviction form B793(ii) from filing cabinet by Miss Weatherby.

TO: Filling Parker pen with Quink Ink in order to write signature.

TO: One sheet blotting paper (A4) for the blottation of the aforementioned above document.

TO: Junior Partner's time licking and affixing stamp (1st Class, £49) to above (½ hour).

TO: Conveyance of same to letterbox by Senior Partner, Sir Geoffrey Perkins, on his way home (1 hour).

TO: Miscellaneous expenses incurred in respect of the above litigation — i.e. travel, stationery, entertainment, clothing, toilet requisites and sundry "impedimenta legalis".

TOTAL: £37,374,287.33p

If this bill is settled within 7 days we'll be really annoyed because we can't charge you interest.

Associated Firms
ALDERSHOT   GLASGOW   JERSEY   MANCHESTER
PARIS   ROME   MOSCOW   SAN FRANCISCO

COOKERY TIPS

Making. Peanut-Butter.

Postman Pat's
CHRISTMAS SURPRISE

"There's a letter for you, Pat," said Mrs Goggins.

"Really?" said Pat. "I wonder if it's a Christmas card."

Pat opened the letter. "Oh dear," he said. "It's a P45."

"Is that bad news, dear?" asked Granny Dryden as Pat began to cry.

"Yes, I've been sacked," sobbed Pat. "What am I going to tell my wife?"

"Tell her you've been rationalised," said Mrs Goggins as she smartened up the Post Office ready for privatisation. "It's the last letter anyone in Greendale will be getting."

So ex-Postman Pat gave back the shiny red van and his smart blue uniform. Then he sat around at home watching Channel 4 racing and *Prime Time* with Maggie Philbin.

Then he went to the pub and spent his redundancy money. There he met Peter Fogg, the farmer.

"Don't moan to me," said Peter. "Under the GATT agreement I've got to set aside most of my farm. I'm less employed than you."

"Never mind, you two," said Granny Dryden, "let's all have a nice cup of vodka."

So ex-Postman Pat staggered back home along the twisty windy roads of Greendale to his home. And there was a message from his wife Sarah on the table.

"Dear Pat, I have left you for Ted Glenn. At least he has a job and he'll be a good father to our black and white cat, Jess."

The Book of Rabin

Chapter One

1. And it came to pass that when Shamir, the leader of the Sons of Israel, had departed hence there came a new leader.

2. And his name was called Rabin, which is to say The Peace-Giver.

3. And, lo, there were dwelling in the land of Israel many Arab-ites and they were known variously as the Araf-ites and the Hamas-ites.

4. And the Hamas-ites and the Araf-ites were divided one against the other, even as the cockroach is unto the dungbeetle.

5. For the Hamas-ites worshipped the God of the Iran-ites and he was called Aya-Tollah.

6. And the Araf-ites worshipped no god save only Yas-ser, he of the tea-towel.

7. Now there rose up certain of the Hamas-ites and did slew one of the Israelites even as he slept.

8. Then the people of Israel did cry aloud with one voice "String 'em up", which is to say "There should be an full enquiry."

9. For the Sons of Israel are merciful even as the day is long.

10. Then Rabin waxed wrath and cryeth: "I am an peaceful man, unlike Shamir who is gone from hence *(see Verse 2)*. Even so, I say unto you, the tribe of Hamas are going to regret this one or my name is not Rabin, son of Rabin."

11. Then he cast forth into the Leb-an-on one hundred men of the Hamas-ites, saying: "Take this blanket and fifty dollars and cometh not back."

12. And so the men of Hamas went forth cursing and shaking the dust from off their boots.

13. But then they came unto Leb-an-on, the Leban-ites said: "No way, José, cometh you here, ye People of Hamas. Be ye gone!"

14. So the Hamas-ites remained in the wilderness, living off locusts and handouts from the people of UN.

15. And the world cried out against Rabin, saying: "Cometh ye back, Shamir! For this Rabin bringeth the sword and treadeth the olive branch beneath his feet.

16. "For, lo! The Araf-ites and the Hamas-ites have long sworn enmity one unto another, but now Rabin hath e'en gone and united them.

17. "Verily, it is like unto the man who kicketh the ball into his own goal upon the field that is called the pitch."

(To be continued)

EXCLUSIVE!

Private Eye has obtained an exclusive copy of Mr Kelvin Mackenzie's Christmas speech delivered at a staff luncheon at El Arso's Restaurant, Wapping, on 23 December 1992.

Cor! What a brilliant year it's been for us lot 'ere at the *Sun*! Oi! You with the tits, Tracy. Get yer T-shirt off and show us wot yer got! *(Raucous cheers)* No, but seriously, *(takes trousers down)* no wonder they call me cheeky! *(Laughter)* and look! *(bends over)* Here's my Anus Horribilis!! *(More laughter, cries of "Good old Kelv!" "What a plonker!" etc)* No, but seriously, I don't know 'bout the Turkey, but we stuffed the Royals!! Ha ha ha. *(Sycophantic laughter from assembled pissed hacks)* And now the loyal toast. Please raise your glasses of lager to His Royal Highness King Murdoch of Filth!! *(Passes out)*

Editor's Note

This speech was obtained through legal means by journalists acting according to the code laid by the PCC — i.e. we stole it and then paid everyone off.

CRICKET'S TOP COUPLE TO SEPARATE

by Our Man In Delhi
Allan Lamb Korma

IT came as a great surprise to no one yesterday that the sport's best-loved couple had agreed on a "non-amicable separation".

Run Out

England captain Graham Gooch and his good-looking blond partner are to split.

Said Graham: "It wasn't working. I wanted to play cricket all the time and David didn't."

David Gower, meanwhile, told a different story. "I wanted our relationship to continue but Graham wouldn't have it. I gave him an ultimatum — choose me or it's all over."

Bombay Duck

Friends of the couple were reported to be very sad. "They should have stayed together for the sake of the runs," said one.

"The worst thing", said another, "is that this business has stopped Graham concentrating on the most important thing in his life — leaving his wife."

Sad Mandy in new slimming shock

by Our Men In The Divorce Courts **Hugh Jaffee and Tiny Settlement**

THERE were gasps in court yesterday as a mysterious slimming disease struck again in the tangled relationship between Miss Mandy Smith, 13, and Mr Bill Wyman, 107.

Stunned observers watched as Ms Bimbo lost millions of pounds in seconds as her waif-like settlement was finally revealed. Once her figure was a stunning 36,24,36 million pounds plus the house. Suddenly her claim was sadly reduced to a painfully thin £500,000.

Crock Star

This tiny fraction of Mr Whyohwhyman's colossal fortune was explained by experts as the result of the syndrome known to doctors as "100 grand per bonk? That's not bad."

The judge, summing up the case, said: "Who is Bill Beaumont?"

Mr Whyohwhyme is 192.

LION TO BE RELEASED INTO THE COMMUNITY

by Our Animal Staff
Zoo Lawley

MRS Virginia Bottomley today announced that the "disturbed" lion at the centre of the Zoogate Affair had been diagnosed as "wild, dangerous and unpredictable".

"This lion", she said, "is a danger to himself and others and there is only one way to deal with him — release him at once."

The Health Minister assured the public that the community would take care of the lion and that it was the only sensible option in the circumstances.

"We can't just lock him up in some decaying Victorian institution, can we?" she concluded.

A senior government spokesman later clarified her comments, saying: "This way the lion will be able to live independently, perhaps find a job, settle down and live a normal life."

Critics, however, suggested that the whole exercise was merely cost-cutting and that it was cheaper to let the lion roam the streets than to care for it properly in a zoo. One psychiatrist said: "There is no doubt about what we are dealing with here. This is a classic case of mental instability. Mrs Bottomley should be put away for the benefit of society as a whole."

The Daily Te LEG raph

Cor! My wife's legs are smashing!

**By the Chairman of the Daily Telegraph
Conrad Blackstockings**

DON'T let the fashion editors tell you that long skirts are great. 'Cos they're not. You can't see a bird's legs when she's wearing a long skirt. What's the point of that? You ask any bloke, like me, whether they want to see their missus in a long or a short skirt. They'll all tell you "Short one so we can see her legs, Conrad."

So I say (and it's my paper so you'd better print it), I say "Shut up about long skirts all you ceuturiers and fashion venduses *(sub: check spelling)* and give us more pictures of leggy crumpet."

Just to prove what I'm saying is right and all the so-called politically corellated *(sub: check)* people in the fashionable Demi-Mondo *(sub: check)* are talking bunk, just look at this bird I married! She's got a great brain and fabulous legs! So, let's look at them! Imagine them wrapped round you of an evening!! Corrr!!

Mrs Conrad Blackstockings (née Amiel)

A bleak outlook

AGAINST the background of the deteriorating situation in war-torn Bosnia, the fragile Somali ceasefire and the virtual collapse of the Middle East Peace Talks, the world as it faces 1993 is looking more unstable than ever.

At home there is more uncertainty, with increasing unemployment and an economy still in the grip of recession and a lack of confidence in both public and private sectors. Rising lawlessness and the failure of previously dependable institutions like the Monarchy have made matters worse.

But amidst all these grave issues, there is surely none more pressing than the tragic attempt of the fashion industry to foist the so-called long skirt upon an unwilling female public. This appalling act of sacrilege, for that is what it is, must be stopped in its tracks, by force if necessary. The UN must insist upon the permanent recognition of the short skirt as the status quo. Mr Boutros Ghali, Lord Owen, President Clinton and John Major must stand firm. They have no greater task this year than the overthrow of the dictators who run the evil fashion empires who seek to *(continued for as long as the Proprietor demands)*

"That's a story that's got legs!"

'Short not long' says legman Black

**By Our Media Staff
Jane Thynne-Legs**

Daily TeLEGraph supremo Conrad Blacktights, 41, has decreed that in future only "short pieces" will be acceptable in his newspapers.

"Nobody wants to see a great long piece," said the Canadian-born sex-fiend, "except when it is written by myself on the subject of skirts. My wife's pieces are very long and tend to taper off at the end. That's why they're in the *Sunday Times*."

Ms Barbara Amiel is 107.

That Frost-Major Interview That Everyone Is Writing About And No One Saw

Sir David: Hullo, good morning and thank you for my knighthood.

Man With Glasses: Thank you for inviting me on your programme.

Sir Frost *(reading autocue)*: Lean forward and smile.

Major: All the classic elements are now in place for a sustained interview to occur.

Sir Frost: My first question, prime minister, is what is a suitable question to ask you first?

Man In Glasses: Now don't try and catch me out!

Frost: Supcr. Ha. Ha. Ha. No but seriously (peering at clipboard) — is it true that you were born in Copenhagen?

Major: You know, Sir David, I read a lot about myself in the papers which I can't believe. Only today they were saying that your knighthood had something to do with this programme.

Sir David: Ha. Ha. Ha. Super.

"You're a changed man since you went to those assertiveness classes, Brian!"

Major: Can I turn now to the subject of the economy? I want to make it clear that we shall go back into the ERM as and when the conditions are right.

Sir Frost: Can I probe a little deeper? What's your name?

Major *(flustered)*: The Princess of Wales would be entirely within her constitutional rights to become Queen. She is the king's husband, and nothing anyone says can alter that fact.

Lord Frost: And now here are Millicent Martin and Lance Percival to sing a song about Mr Beeching's plan to axe the railways.

(Elderly couple come on with small guitar)

Percival & Martin *(for it is they)*:
British Rail is for de chop
All our trains are going to
            stop
Mr Beeching wield his axe
Soon there will be no more
            tracks

Chorus:
Bye bye railway cha-cha
(repeat several times until end of programme)

(Viewer [John Birt] turns off)

On Other Pages

TV Frostie forces Major to admit "I will rejoin ERM"   p.1

"I am no Dane" — Angry Major lashes Frost   p.2

Major weeps under Frost grilling   p.3

Stop this Trial By Tv writes Paul Johnson   p.8

After Sir John Betjeman

Mrs C. Parker-Bowles, Mrs C. Parker-Bowles,
One thrills to the sined of your horse-and-hind vowels.
But, oh! when those trizers go taut as you ride,
One feels an arisal sort of thingy inside.

N.B.

Caught and Circulated

HIGHGROVE

His Royal Highness the Prince of Wales will be calling on Mrs Camilla Parker-Bowles via his hand-held mobile telephonic device. He will open the conversation with a series of smutty innuendoes and will then continue with an informal invitation to fornicate at the home of the Earl of Shelburne. In attendance on the phone will be Duty Officer Perkins from GCHQ, Mrs Stella Rimington of MI5, and Mr Harry Trusslow, a retired bank manager from The Glades, Crawley.

KENSINGTON HOUSE

The Princess of Wales will be receiving ambassadors from the *Daily Sport*, the *Sun* and the *Sunday Times* at an official reception to raise public sympathy for her cause. She will then visit *Hello!* magazine to model her new range of swimwear.

BUCKINGHAM PALACE

The Prince Edward will be receiving a copy of Monday's *Guardian* newspaper in his bedroom and will be examining the "Creative and Media Jobs Vacant" section before formally applying for the post of Deputy Tea Manager at the Slough Community Theatre.

My scoops of 1992

■ Here are just some of the stories that made my Diary the most-read column in the world in 1992...

Jan 7
■ I reveal exclusively that Viscount Linley is thinking of giving up smoking.

Feb 23
■ I disclose the forthcoming engagement of Simon Leigh-Pemberton, 23, the actor-cousin of the Bank of England Governor, and Tracey Redditch, 19, the presenter of Radio Trent's early morning show *Hello Trenties!*

March 3
■ I shock the world with the news that Lord Linley, the Queen's nephew and 33rd in line to the throne, has now gone five days without a cigarette.

April 14
■ I correctly predict that Consuelo Bastardo, a leading figure on the Buenos Aires polo circuit, will be celebrating his 53rd birthday at Evita's in Covent Garden with his third wife Malvina. The chef tells me he is making a special cake for the occasion!

May 3
■ Everyone is astonished by my revelation that Lord Linley, the

brother of Lady Helen Windsor, has been smoking a cigarette at a Covent Garden restaurant. He was guest of honour at the birthday bash for Argentinian playboy Consuelo Bastardo, 57.

June 4
■ To the obvious chagrin of my so-called rivals on various downmarket rags, I disclose the sensational news that well-known actor Simon Leigh-Pemberton has returned from his Caribbean honeymoon with Midlands media star Tracey Redditch "in excellent spirits".

July 28
■ I reveal that Viscount Linley, cousin of Prince Wills, heir to the throne of England, may be thinking of visiting fashionable South American hypnotist Malvina Bastardo in an effort to give up his addiction to nicotine. They met, I report, at a birthday party given in London earlier this year to celebrate Senora Bastarda's husband's 59th birthday.

Aug 4
■ I predict that I will be invited to appear on Radio 2 in the near future, replacing the legendary disc jockey/presenter Ron Clingfilm on his popular midnight-3am show *Sleepy Time*.

Sept 3
■ In my Mustique Diary, much to the rage of down-market rivals, I recount spotting Viscount Linley on the beach. Smoking!

Oct 14
■ To the astonishment of fashionable London, Mario, 47, the longtime chef of chic Covent Garden eaterie Evita's, has walked out in protest against guests smoking between courses. He exclusively assures me, however, that Viscount Linley, 31, cousin of Princess Alice, 91, was not one of the guilty guests who had provoked the biggest furore amongst society diners-out for years.

November 28
■ To the horror of my rivals in the gutter press, I scoop them once again with the news that Simon Leigh-Pemberton, who is no stranger to this column, is to play the part of Prince Bonzo in the pantomime *Puss In Boots* at the Branagh Theatre, Leatherhead. He will share billing honours with TV weatherwoman Suzanne Charlton and Surrey wicketkeeper Kevin Sturrock.

December 24
■ I astonish the world by predicting that tomorrow is Christmas Day.

Scheming and manipulative? Moi?

NO ONE MURDERED SHOCK

by Our Crime Staff **Bill The**

BRITAIN reeled today from the sensational news that no one had been brutally killed for five minutes. Reporters sat in stunned silence as they received the information from police that there had been no shootings, burnings, knifings, joy-riding fatalities or any other form of violent homicides for a record period of three hundred seconds.

The country was further amazed when it was revealed that there had been no rapes, child molestations or kidnaps for most of the same period.

A police spokesman said: "I cannot explain it. I do not know what this country is coming to. We must believe that this is an isolated outbreak in the more normal pattern of British life in the 'nineties."

MAJOR DENIES 'RELATIONSHIP' SHOCK

by Our Alleged Home Affairs Staff
Professor Anthony Clare Latimer

AN ANGRY John Major last night hit out at what he called "scurrilous rumours" linking his name with a Downing Street "cook".

The Prime Minister is to issue writs against the little-read underground paper the *Financial Times*, which this week published a story hinting at a close personal relationship between the Prime Minister and a Mr Norman Lamont.

The allegations, repeated in all other newspapers, suggested that Mr Latimont and Mr Major knew each other "on intimate terms" and had been "seen together" in public on a number of occasions.

Praed Comes Before A Fall

Miss Latimont is a well-known figure in Westminster circles and is highly respected for his ability to cook the books. She is also a familiar figure in West End shopping areas, buying wine she selects herself from importers such as Mr John Onanugu.

Friends described the Prime Minister as "hopping mad" at the smear. His statement claimed: "We have met on a number of occasions in the past, but I hardly know Miss Latimont at all, and after the March reshuffle I hope never to see him again."

That Clare's Kitchen Buffet Lunch Menu in full

Sue of the Day
Platt de Jour

— ❋ —

Alleged Legover of Lamb
with
New Statesman Potatoes and Half-Baked Rumours

— ❋ —

Prime Minister of Steak (Badly Done)
with
Mixed Grilling
— ❋ —
Egg On Face
— ❋ —
Gooseberry Fool
— ❋ —
Hard Cheese served with Writs Crackers

— ❋ —

Humble Pie

— ❋ —

No Dates
Assortment of Humbugs

— ❋ —

To Drink

House of Commons Whine: White or Red-Faced
Major's Not-Very-Sparkling Water
Freshly Groundless Coffee (HAC)

with

Latiamaria Liqueur

"How many ibises are there in 'sphinx'?"

THE Sun

Friday, February 26, 1993

The Sun Says

SORRY
you can't take a joke
MA'AM
(you old bat)

OK, Your Maj. It's a fair cop.

We printed in good faith your Xmas speech. Wot, incidentally, we acquired in a total *bona fide* journalistic scoop — i.e. it was given to us by our mates on Sky TV.

We now realise, after receiving your lawyers' letter, we was wrong to do what we did, even though we was right, because your speech was, frankly, a boring load of bollox, excuse our French, Ma'am.

You have made a right royal gesture by agreeing to hand over some of your ill-gotten loot to the taxman.

And in a similar spirit of vol-

untary cooperation, i.e. we have to, the Sun has generously agreed to publish this apology and fork out a totally ridiculous pile of money to your horse-faced daughter's useless charity.

We hope you are now satisfied with your pound of flesh, Ma'am. But watch out. Cos we've got the dirt on you, hubby, and all the rest of your lot. Gorrit?

Your humble servant

✕   **Kelvin McFilth (his mark)**

"Mr Herriot!"

LETTERS TO THE EDITOR

The moral crisis facing the nation

*From Rt Rev J.C. Flannel,
Archdeacon of Neasden*

Sir, You know it is easy in today's climate of hysteria over so-called juvenile crime to try to find "someone to blame". But, you know, merely pointing the finger at the parents or the criminals themselves helps no one. How much more valid it might be if we were to look beyond the immediate "crimes" which hit the headlines, to the social conditions which have brought them about. When you consider unemployment, inadequate housing, the under-funding of social services, the steady erosion of the welfare state, the emphasis on entrepreneurial capitalism with its "me first" ethic — then is it not clear that the real crime can be laid at the door of ~~Mrs Thatcher~~ John Major.

Yours faithfully,
J.C. FLANGOOD,
YORK.

*From the Archbishop of York,
the Very Rev J.C. Hapless*

Sir, I wish to protest in the strongest possible terms at the way my views have been distorted by the media by the cynical exercise of printing the above letter. I must complain about the printing of that letter, and indeed this one.

Yours faithfully,
J.C. NOGOOD,
Terry's Own Goal,
York.

*From Mr W.F. Deedes
("Oldtimer" of the Morning Post)*

Sir, Talk of "social conditions" by the Archbishop of York and others will not wash down in this neck of the woods.

For those of us who lived through the Thirties, the so-called link between unemployment and crime is so much tommyrot. As a young cub reporter in 1931, I vividly recall visiting one of the most notorious depressed areas in the country. I walked the length and breadth of the Gorbals, where it was not uncommon to find people living 20 to a room, often without a television. But I can assure you that if you happened to drop a gold sovereign in the street, it would not be long before a cheery ragamuffin would hand it back to you with a cheery smile on his grubby face, and a cheeky cry of "Lor' bless you guv'nor".

Yours sincerely,
LORD DEEDESH OF ALDINGTON,
Kent.

From Professor Gunna Blomqvist

Sir, There is nothing new about everything that is happening today. May I remind your readers of the celebrated passage in the 13th century *Gesta Britorum*, written by the monkish chronicler St Ivel of Cornwall.

"Ye young persons of todaye are an ungodly crewe, I witte. They liketh onlie to joyride, as they call it, and to belabour the elder folke of the villages with staves. Licentiousness aboundeth. I blame ye parents and ye clerkes in holie orders. They have faileth to instruct ye younge in ye difference between goode and eville. As ye pagan poetes quoth 'O tempera, O mores'."

Yours obediently,
PROFESSOR HALMAR SCREWLOOSE,
The New University of North Circular (formerly Neasden Polytechnic)

From Ms Fay Weldon

Sir, Today we mourn. We mourn and we grieve. And we mourn. Bobby is dead. And our innocence dies with him. The sheets of Liverpool are awash with our tears. Our tears. Tears of grieving. Because our cities are in chaos. Our morality is in tatters. Our Monarchy is in retreat. And Rushdie is in exile. No wonder we mourn. We mourn the death of the rainforests. We grieve over the whale. Comfort ye my people, as the prophet Salman so rightly said in his masterpiece. And what about the Whips forcing MPs to vote against their consciences in the Maastricht debate? No wonder we mourn. No wonder we grieve.

MORGANA LE FAY WELDON,
Great Drivel,
Glastonbury.

COURT CIRCULAR

The Inauguration of Mrs Hillary Clinton and Her Partner President William Jefferson Airplane III

1st Jogger
The President.

2nd/3rd/4th/5th/6th/7th/8th Joggers
The Presidential Bodyguard.

1st Woman in Trousers
Mrs Hillary Clinton Madonna.

1st Child
Ms Chelsea Town-Hall.

1st Float
The Little Rock Senior High School Prom Swing Band playing a selection of hits from *Hair*.

1st Open Stretch Limo
Mr Michael Jackson, Mr Michael Mouse and Mr Kermit Frog representing "Legendary American Heroes".

1st Open Stretch Coffin
The late Mr Elvis Presley followed by a Grand Procession of Elvis Lookalikes singing "Jailhouse Little Rock".

2nd Open Stretch Limo
The late President Toadthrush and Ms Rosalie-Lurleen Toadthrush.

3rd Open Stretch Limo
Mr Superman III and Ms Batperson, representing more "Legendary American Heroes"

2nd Float
Stars For Clinton, including Ms Jodie Foster. Ms Barbara Streisand, Dr Hannibal Lecter and Mr Darth Vader.

3rd Float
The Native American Community: including Chief Smoking Gun, Chief Smoking Dope, Chief Talking Bull, Chief Ansaphone and Chief Secretary to the Treasury *(surely some mistake? Ed.)*

1st Busload
Washington Afro-American Community representing the City Street Cleansing Department.
(That's enough procession. Ed.)

D O R O T H Y ' S   F R I E N D S

A GROUP of Cambridge graduates who were in the Footlights together meet up to make a film about a group of Cambridge graduates who were in the Footlights together who meet up to make (Get on with it — Ed)

Stephen is a wry, spry Cambridge graduate who lives in a big country house reading P.G. Wodehouse books. He is joined by Hugh, another Cambridge graduate from the Footlights who lives in a slightly smaller house because he's done fewer TV adverts. Meanwhile

Tony, a Cambridge Footlights graduate who now hosts TV shows, arrives with Cambridge Footlights graduate turned screenwriter Martin who has been less successful than the others and ended up with an American wife, Rita.

The fun starts when their old Cambridge Footlights friend Emma brings along her new husband Ken, a successful actor and director who decides to make a film about a group of Cambridge Footlights

(That's enough Cambridge — Ed)

Apology by the Guardian, the Observer and Others

During 1991 we may have given the impression that armed intervention in the affairs of a foreign country, eg Iraq, was an act of imperialistic aggression, indefensible from a moral standpoint. We further argued that stories of human rights abuses by powers such as Iraq could not be used as an excuse to meddle in the internal politics of another state.

We now realise that these sentiments were wholly without foundation of any kind, and we accept that military interference of the most dramatic variety is urgently called for against the Serbian dictator who, in our view, is more evil than Hitler and should be strung up immediately.

HOUSE OF COMMONS
OFFICIAL REPORT

PARLIAMENTARY DEBATES

zzzzzz

HANSARD

The Evidence of Sir Kelvin Mackenzie to the Commons Select Committee on Privacy in the Media

Gyles Brandnew (Pullover, Con): May I begin by asking you, Mr Mackenzie, how you see your role?

Kelvin Mackenzie: My newspaper represents millions of ordinary people wot want to know wot's going on wiv the nobs and the royals an' that an' they want to 'ave a bit of a larf in the mornings. Wot's wrong wiv that?

Gyles Brandnew: Thank you very much indeed.

Joe Washedup (Ee-by-Gumme, Lab): Ordinary folk like me 'appen as 'ad enough of thy paper with its invasion into t'lives of ordinary old-age pensioners like me.

Macfilth: Come off it, mate! Look 'oo's talking! You used to write a load of bollocks in the *Daily Star* yourself! 'Ere, I've got photocopies if you want a look.

Ashenface: Thank you very much indeed.

Sir Gerald Kaufperson (Oklahoma! Lab): Many people regard your newspaper with utter contempt. How would you like it if photographers came to your house and tried to…

Kelvin McBlackmail: Look matey I've got the goods on you so you'd better wind yer neck in or you'll be on the front page! And you know what the headline will be, don't you, sweetie-pie?

Kaufperson: I see. Thank you very much.

McBlackmail: All you lot want me to do is shut up abaht wot you're up to. I know everything about every one of you!! (*Points finger round room*)

All: Thank you.

McBlackmail: But I'm no respecter of persons, no way. The rich an' powerful don't put the wind up me. I don't suck up to no one. (*Portable phone rings*) Hello, Mr Murdoch, sir. It's going fine. Yes, sir, yes, sir. Amen, sir. God bless Your Majesty and long live Your Holiness. (*Continues for several hours*)

"More 'E', Vicar?"

by Philip Howard

PIMLOTT
n. A very long, tedious book about some long-forgotten Labour politician that no-one will ever want to read. Example: "Just throw another pimlott on the fire will you, darling."

DEGSY
n. Liverpudlian slang. A wide boy, spiv, Jack-the-lad. One who gets away with it. Example: "Our wacker's a reet degsy" (The Collected Poems of Roger McGough).

CAMILLEPAGLIA
n. (Italian). Gibberish; high-flown nonsense involving academic and cultural references. Example: "I have never heard such camillepaglia in all my life."

HUSSEY
v. trans. To hurry through something rather shady in the hope that no one will notice. Example: "The chairman husseyed it through during the tea break."

BOTTOMLEY
adv. In a priggish manner designed to convey the impression that all is going well when one is presiding over a disaster. Example: "She announced the hospital closures very bottomley indeed" (Hansard 1993). Old English *bumley*.

SHERRIN
n. Very old theatrical anecdote, probably made up. Example: "Oh no, not that old sherrin again, please."

PALIN
n. a humourless and long-winded traveller, one prone to talk at inordinate length about his experiences in foreign parts. Example: "There was an awful palin at dinner last night, going on about his trip to the North Pole."

GREER
v. int. to lecture, berate, pontificate, often for hours at a time. (Australian) Example: "She greered on all day, until I could take no more."

PORTILLO
n. man who builds up inflated reputation by staying silent. Example: "Don't be fooled — he's just a portillo." (From *Pomp and Prejudice*, J. Austen)

"It's quite tragic the way they've been westernised"

TOP HOLLYWOOD STARS SAY 'NO' TO VIOLENCE

by Kim Bashingheroverthehead

TWO of Hollywood's leading actors have joined in the new crusade for a less violent cinema, it was announced last night.

Both 50-year-old Tom and co-star Jerry, 50, have intimated that they may not make any more sequels to their highly successful "Tom and Jerry" movies.

Said Tom: "I now realise that what we as performers do on the screen does have an identifiable effect on the standards of behaviour, especially of the young, in society as a whole. As an artist, I do feel responsible."

His remarks were echoed by his co-star Jerry, who has been involved in what he described himself as "some of the most horrifically violent scenes ever filmed."

He said that he now recoils in horror at one particular scene in which he stuffed a lighted stick of dynamite in Tom's mouth and laughed as it blew up.

Hannibal Lecture

But this was nothing, said Tom, compared with the infamous sequence in *Jerry Gets a Shock* (1957), when Tom administered 2,000 volts to Jerry's brain and then beat his blackened and burnt body re-

peatedly with a spade until the mouse was totally flat.

"We just took the money and the awards," admitted the shamefaced duo, "but now we are determined to get some publicity along with everyone else. Our next film, which is currently in pre-production, will tell the story of a cat and a mouse who learn to live in harmony across the barriers of species, class and race."

LATE NEWS

MORE HOLLYWOOD IMMORTALS JOIN 'SAY NO' CAMPAIGN

New names that have today publicly pledged their support for Tom and Jerry's stance include Sylvester the Cat, Tweety Pie, Bugs Bunny, the Roadrunner, Wile E. Coyote, Popeye and Postman Pat *(shurely shome mishtake? Ed)*.

(Reuters)

Preview

Virgin Radio
What You Will Hear

9.00 am *Come Fly With Me*   Frank Sinatra

9.01 am *No, Come Fly With Me, It's Cheaper*

                                                   Lord King

(That's enough Branson. Ed.)

WHAT EVERYONE WANTS TO KNOW ABOUT THE GOVERNMENT'S PLANS TO REVOLUTIONISE BRITISH RAIL

Mr MacGregor answers your questions

Q. Is British Rail going to be privatised?

A. Yes and no. Yes if you approve and no if you don't.

Q. Can you explain?

A. It's quite simple really. Our proposal is to separate British Rail into a number of component sectors. For example, most of the track will remain the responsibility of British Rail.

Q. So British Rail will still exist?

A. Well, not in its present form. The old BR will become an independent franchised agency, regulated by Offrail, which is what most of the trains will be.

Q. What about the signalling system?

A. The signals will be operated by a new commercial agency called Signalforce, who will lease the signals from Trackforce, the new track operation.

Q. What about British Rail sandwiches?

A. I wouldn't touch them with a bargepole if I was you, since they were redesigned by that Clement Freud. His Kumquat 'n' Bacon Experience is definitely one to be missed.

Q. No, what I meant was — will they be called 'Sandwichforce'?

A. Stations will be known as

Tieracks, and trains, run by the new franchises such as British Airways, Good Morning TV and Spud-U-Like, will operate whenever they can get enough passengers to make a lot of money.

Q. Will fares come down?

A. Yes.

Q. You must be joking.

A. I am, ha, ha, ha.

Q. Under your new scheme, how would you get from, say Brighton to London?

A. Very simple. First you would go down to Brighton Tierack, and catch a new Virgin Downsline to Hastings. There you would connect with the World of Weald system, which would take you across to Maidstone. Then you would jump on one of the new Whitecliffs Express shuttles which would get you to Dover in plenty of time for tea. Then, if you still wanted to get to London, you could nip over on the Hovercraft to France, where it would only take you an hour on their very good, cheap state system to reach Paris. Then it's a piece of cake to hop on a plane to Heathrow, and there you are. What could be easier?

Q. Why don't you resign, Mr MacGregor?

A. You will be hearing from my solicitors.

WHAT EVERYONE WANTS TO KNOW ABOUT THE GOVERNMENT'S PLANS TO REVOLUTIONISE BRITISH MAIL

Mr Heseltine explains

Q. How will it work?

A. It won't.

Q. So why are you doing it?

A. What happens is that I close the pits down, and then open them up again.

Q. And then what?

A. I come up with an even worse idea.

Q. Could we get back to your plans to ruin the postal services?

A. Stampforce... franchise... hive-off... Jiffybagforce... queueforce... Closed on Wednesdaysforce... commercialise... rationalise...

vast profits... no one writes letters any more, they just send faxes... er... that's it.

"British Rail apologise for the late arrival of the..."

MIKE TURNER

THAT BIRT TAX RETURN IN FULL

1. Name Of Company — John Birt Management & Consultancy Services Ltd

2. Company Address — 214 Eldorado Crescent, London SE94

3. Directors' Full Names — John Complete Birt
Emmie-Lou Birt (wife)
Marmaduke Birt (dog)

4. Purpose of Company — (i) To furnish, develop and otherwise provide consultancy, administrative and resource management services in the audio-visual field.
(ii) To avoid tax.

5. Total Revenue 1991/2 — £486,212.04 (paid on "Marmgus No. 1" Account, Cayman Islands Bank, per pro The British Broadcasting Corporation.

6. Total Expenses 1991/2 £486,212.06

Breakdown of non-taxable outgoings and allowances

Secretarial help (Mrs E-L. Birt)	£47,413
Dogfood (M. Birt)	£5,414
Silly glasses	£46,415
Imported suits	£5,449
Mr Birt's hairdressing	£17,450
Aromatherapy	£3,451
Bereavement counselling (Eldorado)	£4,453
Pizza-to-go	£11,456
Paper clips	£51,459
Satellite TV installation (Sky)	£61,466
Phone calls to Mr Murdoch	£26,467
1 copy "How To Make Friends & Influence People" (with introduction by Sir D. Frost)	£4,482
Financial advice (P. Jay)	£13,488
Dental floss	£26,491
Rostrum Camera (Ken Morse)	£54,503
Mortgage repayments	£41,537
Sundry freebies	£212,595

I Certify That The Above Constitutes A True And Faithful Account Of The Expenses Incurred By The Company In Its Efforts To Minimise Its Tax Liability.

Signed

Marmaduke Hussy

M. HUSSEY
pp Board of Governors

"I'd love to stay and listen to this fascinating conversation all night, gentlemen, but unfortunately I have to wind it up now and go to bed"

BBC RADIO FOUR

Highlights

9.05am Call Nick Ross
Listeners are invited to ring in with their views on the burning moral issue of the day — should John Birt resign? Nick says no.

10.00am Prayer For Today
Director-General John Birt offers prayers of intercession to keep his job.

10.15am Money Box
Louise Botting asks: "Are you paying too much tax?" She talks to business consultant J. Birt on how going self-employed could save you £800 a year.

10.16am Armani Box
Selina Scott looks at the world of male fashion and shows how you can afford Italian suits by going on Schedule D.

10.30am Woman's Hour
Jenni Murray talks about the problems of combining the roles of company director and secretary with staying at home looking after the children. Today's guest: Ms Emmie-Lou Birt.

11.15am Morning Story
John Birt tells a delightful fairy tale about his income tax.

12.30pm Face The Facts
Radio 4 examines why the Inland Revenue turns a blind eye to obvious fiddles by senior company executives.

**2.00pm
Famous For 15 Minutes**
Ex-jailbird Mark Henshaw was an obscure accountant when suddenly he found himself in the national spotlight as John Birt's personal financial adviser.

**2.45pm
The Auditors (serial)**
An everyday story of accountancy folk. This week Ernst and Young are worried about John's clothing allowance. Will the Revenue wear it?

**4.05pm
Does He Take The Blame?**
Programme for the disabled. How can we improve the image of people without a leg to stand on? Guest: Sir Marmalade Gussett, former Chairman of the BBC.

**5.30pm
I'm Sorry, I Haven't A Clue**
A panel of BBC Governors give humorous excuses as to why they let Birt and Hussey get away with it.

**11.15pm
Crook At Bedtime**
Economics editor Peter Jay pays tribute to his former employer Robert Maxwell — "a man of great moral and physical courage".

**11.30pm
Shopping Forecast**
Various senior members of the BBC shop John Birt — or not, as the case may be.

11.45pm Closedown
of BBC.

BBC NEWS AT NINE

NEWSREADER *(Martyn Lewis, for it is he):* The main news today is that I support my boss John Birt. And so do many of my colleagues. For a full report on the growing tide of support for John Birt, over to our Economics Editor Peter Jay…

JAY: Forget about this afternoon's Budget — the big story of the day is how I've come out in support of my old friend John Birt.

(Cut to graph showing how Jay's salary has risen by 400 per cent under Birt)

LEWIS: Now, for another special report on today's main story, our Social Affairs Editor Polly Technic (now the University of Toynbee)…

TOYNBEE (outside Job Centre): This is the one place John Birt shouldn't be. *(Cut to film of worried ex-BBC employees looking at boards)* You won't find any of these cards advertising a vacancy for Director-General of the BBC. That's because it takes a man of extraordinary vision, honesty and leadership qualities to give me a regular slot droning on every night.

LEWIS: And news is just coming in that Polly Technic, the widely respected Social Affairs Editor of the BBC, has thrown her weight behind the growing campaign to keep John Birt in office. But now, for the political dimension to this crisis, over to our Political Editor Robin Oakley, at Westminster…

OAKLEY: Some MPs here at Westminster may still be debating the Maastricht Treaty. But the real question in the corridors of the Palace of Westminster tonight is whether I support John Birt in his gallant fight to hold on to his job. And the answer has to be an unqualified yes.

LEWIS: And now today's Foreign News…

(Film of John Simpson next to UN tank in Sarajevo)

SIMPSON: I support John Birt all the way. Goodnight.

LEWIS: Thank you, John. And now tomorrow's weather from Ian McCaskill…

SMALL EXCITABLE SCOTS PERSON WITH GLASSES: Hullo. Well, there's a cloud over John Birt at the moment, but it's not going to last. During the week it'll move slowly away and settle over Hussey. Quite right, too. Good night.

CONTINUITY: And now Peter Sissons tells us what's in store on *Question Time* later this evening.

SISSONS: My guests tonight are Mr Will Wyatt, Mr David Hatch, Ms Liz Forgan and someone else who owes their vast salary to John Birt. And we'll be agreeing that Mr Birt should stay on in his job. Yes, you sir, the man in the expensive suit and the glasses.

Come off it, Birt!!

writes **Lunchtime O'Booze**

© All newspapers

THE sickening spectacle of a man fiddling his expenses is almost too sickening to contemplate.

Especially when he occupies a prominent position in the media.

Come off it, Birt!

The public have a right to expect the highest moral standards from those who work in the media.

That is why every right-thinking journalist on Fleet Street joins me in saying today — John Birt must go.

```
        Memo to Editor

    Hope this will do. I enclose note on my exes for
this piece:

        To Expenses on Birt Feature

Lunch with imaginary Senior BBC Contact    £300.00
                                           £552.00
Drinks with media sources
                                           £720.00
Taxis to and from above

New suit for interviewing Marmaduke        £460.00
Gussett (interview cancelled, suit kept)
                                           £121.00
Petrol (for taxi)
                                        £21,612.00
TOTAL
```

cheers!
L. O'B

BIRT TO JOIN BBC

by Our Media Staff **Jeremy Taxman**

A FREELANCE TV producer, John Birt, 48, is to join the staff of the BBC, much to the surprise of himself.

Birt, who had previously been "helping out" the BBC as a full-time Director General, said: "There is nothing dishonest or underhand about my previous tax arrangements, which is why, now I have been caught out, I am changing them immediately."

Mr Birt's employer, Sir Marmalade Gussett, said: "We are delighted to have Mr Birt on the team. He has a first-rate tax accountant *(shurely 'mind'? Ed)* and will make a valuable contribution to the Inland Revenue *(shurely 'programming standards'? Ed).*

"We've had successful solo careers but we all felt the time was right for us to start working as a group again"

Le Darling Buds of Mayle

(par Mayles Kington)

(Silly French accordion music)

INSPECTOR MORSE *(pour c'est lui)*: Ah, ici nous sommes in Provence. Ah, le food! Le vin! Le brandy! Et les tres amusants French locals, avec ses mosutaches et le fameux beret!

SGT LEWIS: Sir, I do not understand what you are on about. Ou est le body dans cet case?

POIROT: Ah, zere you 'ave me, 'astings. *(Surely quelque erreur? Ed.)*

1st FRENCH PERSON: 'Allo, 'allo — I shall say zees only once.

EVERYONE: Non, you won't — you 'ave to spin it out for 12 episodes.

MORSE: Ah, ca c'est la true mystere! 'Own can zees tres thin libre be strung out comme les oignons sur la bicyclette?

FAT POLICE CHIEF: Morse, I want de vous voir in mon office immediatement. You are charged with impersonating a retired advertising executive. Comment pleadez-vous?

MORSE: J'ai besoin de la monnaire.

SGT LEWIS: Rubbish, sir.

MADAME MAYLE: Ha, ha, ha.

(More silly accordion music. Loving shots of Provençal countryside)

CREDITS

None, except Rostrum Cameraman Inspector Ken Morse

"And you'll love the neighbours – they're dead!"

Notes & Queries

A service by our readers for our readers (as seen in all other newspapers)

QUESTION: Why do giraffes have long necks?

ORIGINALLY the giraffe, or Giraffus giraffus africanus, looked more like a small sheep but during the Jurassic Period (9-8 million years BC) it evolved into the long-necked creature we know today. — *D. Attenborough, c/o BBC.*

QUESTION: Who wore the first bowtie?

THE first recorded wearer of a bowtie was Sir Farquharson "Beau" Tighe (1787-1861), who was seen at the Brighton Pavilion in May 1808 in what was described in the *Spectator* as "a perfectly ghastly pink cravat incorrectly knotted in the middle". Despite the *Spectator*'s strictures, Sir Farquharson's innovation quickly set a fashion which has survived to this day. — *P.B. Smithiers, Rutland Cravat Co.*

QUESTION: Is it true that Hitler liked sausages?

THERE is no written evidence that Hitler ever ate a sausage, although sausages have long been popular in Bavaria, the part of Germany in which Hitler lived from 1921 to 1924. — *D. Irving, author of 'Hats Off To Hitler' (Sinclair-Stevenson).*

QUESTION: How can you weigh your own nose?

CONTRARY to B.L. Chevenix-Trench's strange assertion last week that the weight of a nose can be calculated according to the formula

$$\frac{a - b}{L} \, (\, c \,) = x$$

where a = the overall weight of the body, b = the volume of water displaced by nose in bath, c = the volumetric weight of the bathwater and L = the VAT registration number, might I offer a simpler solution? *(No. Ed.)*

QUESTION: Why do we sleep lying down?

A RECENT study published by the Institute de Sommeil in Limoges showed that the prone position for sleep is by no means universal. The Waki-Waki islanders in Melanesia sleep standing on their heads with no ill-effects. — *Baroness Blackstone, Birkbeck College.*

NEXT WEEK: Answers please to the following: What does the "A.N." stand for in A.N. Wilson? Do bats dream? Where does the saying "fit as a fiddle" come from? Why do people buy the *Sunday Times*?

TV

Both Feet in the Grave

(Various Times)

William Rees-Mogg, the nation's favourite misery guts, is back in a hilarious new series of articles! William rants and raves about the 20th Century, the strength of the Deutschmark and the need for a return to spirituality before

the forthcoming end of the world.

Victor Rees-Meldrew	Richard Wilson
Lady Rees-Meldrew	Annette Crosbie
TV's Charles Moore	
	TV's Angus Deayton

SUPERSTAR DENIES CHANGING COLOUR

by Our Showbiz Correspondent
Oprah Bamigboye

IN a heartrending television interview, internationally unknown superstar "Not Very Wacko" John Smith denied that he has deliberately changed colour over the last ten years.

He angrily hit out at media speculation that he turned from a normal pink to an almost unnatural deep blue.

Non Thriller

"I can't help it," he said. "It's a hereditary disease called Losing-thelectionitis which afflicts all leaders of the Labour party."

Sobbing uncontrollably into his onion, the uneccentric Scottish lawyer said:

"It's all lies. I'm proud to be a red man. I love our culture, our music, our voter. I have no desire to be blue."

At one point Oprah suggested that John Smith might in fact be mad, living in a fantasy world in Walworth Road with his pet monkey Gordon Brown.

John Smith was clearly embarrassed and turned an even deeper shade of blue.

Skinner Complaint

But fireworks really flew when the conversation turned to cosmetic surgery. Oprah claimed:

BEFORE

In the days of "Benn"

AFTER

During "Loonwalk"

At this John Smith completely lost his temper and insisted that from then on he only wanted to talk about his record, "I'm Bad".

Oprah Winfrey is 78 stone.

"You've reshaped your policies, had your left wing removed, 'tucked' Gerald Kaufman away, and implanted conservatism into your body politic."

THE INVISIBLE MAN

starring John Smith

An extraordinary story about a man who becomes invisible after an experiment in choosing a new leader goes horribly wrong. Amazing special effects include John Smith fuming at the fact that no-one listens to him.

Co-starring Tony Blair as The All Too Visible Man and Roy Hattersley as The Risible Man. *(That's enough Men — Ed.)*

NEW WORDS

by Philip Howard

BIRT
n. Bureaucratic jargon, corporate nonsense, meaningless verbiage, drivel. Example: "That man in glasses is talking absolute birt."

FORGAN
n. Successful career woman with talent for listening to birt. Example: "She'll get the job all right — she's a forgan." (From *BBC Handbook*, **1993**.)

KELLNER
n. person who is invariably wrong in his predictions; e.g. "You stupid kellner — you said it would be a nice day and we got soaked" (coll.)

BLUNKETT
vb. int. to waffle; e.g. "He blunketted on all evening" (source — *Hansard*)

BRUNO
n. a traditional pantomime character; e.g. "Enter Bruno *(audience cheers wildly for 10 minutes)*." See also: Botham.

WOGAN
n. living zombie; one of the undead; Irish mythological being; e.g. "Watch out, or the wogan'll get you." (W.B. Yeats, *Noddy and the Goblins*)

BRAGG
n. (regional slang, orig. fr. Cumbria and Hampstead); the act of sexual congress between a middle-aged man and a much younger woman. Example: " 'appen tha's a feisty lass. Fancy a bragg?" (from *The Crystal Balls* by Melvyn Bonk).

PAXMAN
n. a superior, supercilious sort of person. One who cannot speak without sneering, as in: "Did you see that bloody paxman last night? The poor Croatian deputy-foreign minister couldn't get a word in edgeways."

FERGIE
n. a fleeting, inconsequential sexual relationship, as in: "It wasn't a big deal, it was just a fergie." (prob. derived from Anglo-Saxon verb "to ferg", cogn. with Old French "bonque").

Critics acclaim return of Maggie

The Importance Of Being In The ERM

by Lunchtime O'Wilde

(Scene: a drawing room in Downing Street. A young man in glasses is pacing nervously up and down, as if he is expecting an important visitor. There is an imperious knock at the door. Enter LADY THATCHER)

JOHN MAJOR *(for it is he):* Ah, Lady Thatcher. I can explain everything.

DAME MAGGIE: To lose one Commons vote might be counted a misfortune. To lose two makes you look like a twit.

MAJOR: I was only trying to emulate you, Lady Thatcher.

MAGGIE: I see. A case of the unspeakable in full pursuit of the unbeatable.

MAJOR: I hear that poor Lord Ridley has died.

MAGGIE: How could he, after all I did for him?

(Awkward pause)

MAJOR *(offering her a cucumber sandwich):* May I enquire how you are spending your time these days?

DAME MAGGIE: I am reading my memoirs. It is so important to have something really boring to read on the train. Not

that I ever travel by train, you recall.

MAJOR: But I'm going to privatise the trains.

THATCHER: That is the one mistake I never made.

(Hits him with handbag)

MAJOR: A handbag!

(Curtain. For Major)

Cast in full

Lady Thatcher   **Maggie Smith**
An Ideal Husband

Denis Thatcher
A Woman of No Importance

Claire Lattimer
Lady Thatcher's Fan

Charles Moore

ICARUS WOZ HERE

NOMA

THE PRISONER

The cult TV show brought to you by Group 4 Security

(Silly 'sixties music)

NUMBER ONE: Bring in the Prisoner! Bring in Number Six!

NUMBER TWO: I'm afraid he has escaped, sir.

NUMBER ONE: But Number Four was meant to be guarding him!

NUMBER TWO: Yes, but he lost him.

NUMBER ONE: Why?

NUMBER TWO: Er... I'm sorry... The reason escapes me

(Silly closeup on Number One's face)

NUMBER ONE: Right, Number Two. I'm holding you responsible... Number Two? Number Two? Where have you gone?

(Cut to Number Six strolling happily outside high wall)

NUMBER SIX: I am not a number. I'm a Free Man!

NUMBERS SEVEN TO 394: Join the club!

(More silly music. Ends.)
© Channel Group Four

St Cake's

Forgan Term begins today. There are 862 boys in the school and 83 girls, most of them pregnant owing to the unusual events that took place in a disused hangar one night last July, and which earned the school welcome publicity in the *News of the World* under the headline "YES — IT'S ST CRACK'S". J. Armani-Suit (Birt's) is Chief Tax Dodger and Miss Janet Street-Cred (Porter's) is Senior Yoof. Mr Marmaduke Gusset has been invited by the Governors to stay on as Headmaster for a further term of 15 years. Mr M. Checkland has

been asked to retire as the school accountant after the loss of £60 million. Mr A.P. St.J. Botney has become Head of Paxman's. The Perks will be run over Wyatt's Lawn on 15 June. The Founder's Day Sermon, on the theme "That's Life", will be preached in the Chapel by the Deaconess E. Rantzen-Wilcox. The play will be *A Year In Provence*, specially adapted for the school by P.F.B. Mayle (OC). Eldorado's will be on 1 July. The annual OC Dinner and Dance will be held in the BBC Canteen, Wood Lane, on 25 July. Tickets from the bursar Col. S.R.B. Milosevic, The Bunker, Belgrade.

God to leave Church of England

by The Word Staff **Terry Christian**

FOLLOWING the precedent set by leading former Anglicans, God has indicated that he too is to leave the Church of England.

Friends of God believe the issue of women priests to have been behind the Almighty's sudden decision to convert to Rome and say that he may well have been persuaded by the arguments of the agriculture minister and pond expert Mr Gummer.

According to sources close to God (TV's Charles Moore), He has been unhappy for some time with the direction the Anglican Church has been taking, and has now finally had enough.

He will be accepted into the Catholic Church on condition that he takes instruction from an expert theologian who can explain His beliefs to Him properly.

A CofE spokesman said: "Losing God is a bit of a blow but after major figures like Anne Widdecombe defecting it's just something we're going to have to live with."

BLUE PETER PRESENTER SPLITS WITH DARLING BUDS STAR

...and here's one I laid earlier

The Alternative Rocky Horror Service Book

No. 94. A Special Service For The Reception Of An Member Of Her Majesty's Government Into The Roman Catholic Church

The President: Brothers and Sisters, we are gathered here today to welcome our new convert (N or MP) who has freely, of his or her own will, renounced the C of E and all its works.

All: Especially those ghastly women priests.

President: Did you see that one on the telly?

All: Yes we did. Wasn't she awful?

The candidate shall then present himself (or it might be herself) before the President.

President: Do you turn away from Carey and all his heresies?

Candidate: I do, indeedy.

President: Do you abhor the iniquities of Habgood?

Candidate: I refer my right honourable friend to the answer I gave previously.

All: Resign, resign.

President: Order, order.

There shall then be a Reading from the First Book of Gummermiah.

"And there was a certain poor man who dwelt in the land of the Suffolk-ites. And round about him was a garden in which all manner of tares and thistles had sprung up. And his pond was dried up and barren. Nor was there any frog or newt that dwelleth therein.

And, lo, while he slept, there was an miracle. His pond filled with clear water, like unto the brook Shiloh.

Then the poor man rejoiced and gave thanks, even unto Hillsdown Holdings plc who had brought this mighty thing to pass, out of the goodness of their hearts and with no thought of the commercial advantages that might accrue unto them therefrom."

President: Here endeth the reading of the Parable of the Pond.

All: Thanks be to Gummer.

THE INDUCTION

At this point the media may be brought in to witness the Act of Faith. If there shall be any photographers present, the President shall invite them up to the altar for an close-up.

Photographers: Over here, Anne. (Or they may say "Give us a smile, love — can we have a bit of leg?")

The President: Do you acknowledge the Pope is the Supreme Pontiff of the Catholic and Apostolic Church.

Candidate: I refer the honourable President to the press statement which I issued on — (here he or she shall name the date), in which I set out my policy with regard to this one very clearly, and, if I may say so, very fully.

All: Answer, answer.

Candidate: I will not give way.

President: Do you accept the following doctrines? The Infallibility of the Pope, the Treaty of Rome, the Forgiveness of Synods and Proportional Transubsidiarity?

Candidate: I am sure, my honourable friend, that there is much to be said on both sides of all these important questions.

All: You're not in the Church of England now.

There shall then be sung the Te Dium, followed by a celebration of Masstricht.

DISMISSAL

The President: The poor old C of E's rather washed up, isn't it?

All: Yeah.

The President: There's no place like Rome.

All shall now depart to watch ceremony on News At Six.

Introducing our new £50,000-a-minute star columnist

ANNE DIABOLICAL

Why you should watch me on TV

Me on TV

I WAS walking down the street the other day when hundreds of people came up and asked me for my autograph. It's really great being on telly!

Mum's the word

I am a mother and yet I appear on TV in the mornings. Is it possible for a woman to combine both roles? And, what's more, to write a column in the *Daily Mirror*?

Well, all I can say is — *I* do it. But then I am brilliant!

Anne other one

I WAS walking down the street on the way to the supermarket (having returned from the TV studio) when an old man said to me: "Aren't you Anne Robinson?"

Anne Robinson, with all due respect, can't write a column and looks terrible on television. How could anyone possibly confuse us?

Aren't some people stupid?

NEXT WEEK: More of the same.

"The self-hanging portrait — you're a genius, da Vinci!"

ON THE AIR

The Today Programme
Radio Four

SUE McGREGOR *(for it is she):* ...thank you very much, Chief Rabbi — and now Bosnia. On the line from Tuzla we have a Canadian aid worker who is going to give us an extremely horrific and disturbing eye-witness account of what really happened in last week's massacre. I must warn listeners in advance that the questions I am going to ask are so shocking that many people will be utterly revolted.

CANADIAN VOICE: Hullo.

McGREGOR: Could you describe for us in detail exactly what you saw last week when all the women and children were killed? I mean, was there a great deal of blood? Did you see children actually dying in front of your eyes? I'm afraid we haven't got a great deal of time, so could you describe for our listeners the very worst and most heartrending things you saw — we only have five seconds, I'm afraid, so could you pick out the most gruesome and sickening incident of all?

VOICE: Er...

McGREGOR: ...well, thank you, for that really horrendous picture of what it is like to see people being blown up. And now, Paul McCartney at 51. Do you remember this tune...

(Sound of old Beatles record)

GENERALS SAY NO TO WAR

by Our Defence Editor
Brig. Harry Trumper-Smythe

■ **NATO's top generals hit out yesterday at what they called "the ludicrous idea" that they should be asked to fight in Bosnia.**

"What these people don't realise," said General Sir John Weasel, "is that war is a jolly dangerous business. You can get shot at, you know. People might even be killed."

His views were echoed by US General Colin Hackenbush III. "What do these politicians think they're playing at," he thundered. "I didn't join the army to go into battle. That sort of thing was all very well in the past, but it's quite out of place for the modern soldier."

Brig. Trumper-Smythe comments:

The view put over by NATO's top strategists yesterday accords with the latest doctrines of NCW or non-combatant warfare, as I outlined in my recent book *Hands Up, We Surrender*. The role of the soldier in the post-Cold War period is to act as an observer while various foreigners massacre each other. The old-fashioned notion of using a highly trained and expensively equipped force to take part in an armed conflict is now generally viewed as a wasteful and inappropriate use of resources.

A Doctor Radovan Karadzic Writes

As a mass murderer I am often asked: "Does signing a peace treaty bind me to an international agreement?"

The simple answer is "no". What happens is that the doctor, in this case myself, exhibits psychopathic tendencies mixed with delusions of grandeur or, as we doctors call it, *Serbianis bastarditis abnormalis*.

The only remedy is to threaten to bomb the doctor into oblivion and then try him for war crimes. This may then have the welcome side-effect of the Doctor pretending to be a reasonable human being again.

© *A Doctor Owen 1993*

NEW TEST FOR 14-YEAR-OLDS

by Our Education Staff **N.U.T. Case**

A NEW test has been introduced for all 14-year-olds to "assess their general performance and competence across a wide range of disciplines".

In a trial run carried out on one particular 14-year-old, however, the results were startling.

The teenager in question, H.M. Government, was found to have "learned absolutely nothing" in the past 14 years.

The examinee received the following report:

Mathematics: 0 per cent. Can't even count.

Geography: 0 per cent. Thought "Bosnia" was a type of lager.

Reading: 0 per cent. Had not read Maastricht Treaty before signing it.

Domestic Science: 0 per cent. Did not know the cook.

History: 0 per cent. Blamed Labour Party for everything.

Creative Writing: 0 per cent. Has written a number of Charters and a few budgets, all showing no promise.

Comments: Could not do worse.

Having studied the report, Mr John Patten said that this type of testing was "totally unacceptable". He called for "continuous assessment," or better still "no assessment at all" as the fairest means of enabling the Government to stay in power.

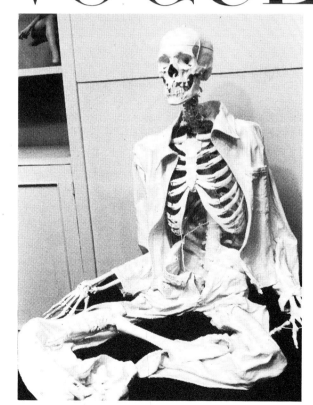

GOVERNMENT STICKS TO POLICY SHOCK

by Our Political Staff **Simon Hefferlump**

IN AN extraordinary about-turn last night the Government committed itself to sticking firmly to one of its policies.

There was outrage in the Commons when Prime Minister Major announced his unwavering dedication to the central plank of the Government's political strategy — the U-turn.

"I have said that we will do U-turns and U-turns is what we will do. We'll do them before breakfast, before lunch and before dinner. There is no room for argument."

He continued to address his open-mouthed backbenchers with a firm, resolute and statesmanlike delivery.

"The people of this country expect consistency from us and that's what they will get. We will announce policies and then immediately abandon them. Every time. And that is a promise."

The Laddy's Not For Turning

As the initial response to his policy statement proved unfavourable (one Member shouting "Shame!" and another whispering "I'm not sure what the *Telegraph* will think of this") Mr Major hurriedly added:

"My Government will do U-turns on everything. Including the U-Turn Policy I've just announced, which I am now abandoning. Unless anyone objects. Goodnight."

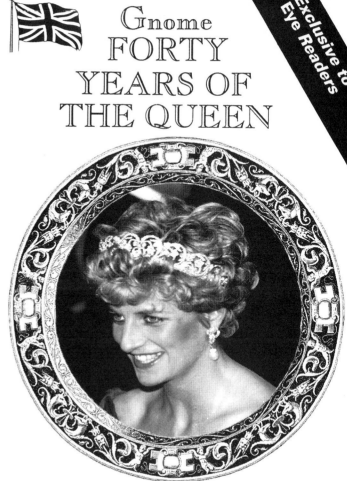

HOSPITAL KILLER –
Public demands full enquiry

by Our Health Staff **Sir Barts Simpson**

FURIOUS victims yesterday called for a full public enquiry into the case of the serial killer who cold-bloodedly murdered many of Britain's best-known hospitals.

Virginia Bottomley, who for legal reasons cannot be named, was given a job "way beyond her capabilities and for which she was entirely unsuited", the court heard.

As soon as she was appointed as Health Secretary in 1992, innocent hospitals began to suffer mysterious attacks, many of which proved fatal.

Although suspicions began to be raised about Mrs Bottomley's part in the serial killings, no one saw fit to remove her from her job.

Her boss, Mr Major, even went out of his way to say that she was "doing a wonderful job", at the very time when the death toll was rising rapidly.

Black Bottomley

Now, finally, questions are being asked about the role of the authorities in allowing this mad axe-woman to run amok in the country's hospitals.

The Government has set up a full private enquiry under Sir Cecil Whitewash to establish Mrs Bottomley's complete innocence.

In his report, published last year, Sir Cecil will find that Mrs Bottomley suffered from a rare psychic disorder known as Majorhausen's Disease.

Victims of this syndrome live in a dream state, and have no idea what is going on in the real world.

The victims of this disease are almost always members of the Cabinet.

THOSE 10 ASIL NADIR CONDITIONS IN FULL

I, Asil Nadir, agree to return to the United Kingdom on the following conditions:

1. **That I will be given a fair trial in a British court and found innocent.**

2. **That I shall be awarded full compensation for the loss of other people's money.**

3. **That the Serious Fraud Office will apologise to me personally on their knees for suggesting that I might in any way be dishonest or fraudulent.**

4. **That all British media should be closed down as a fitting and proper penalty for all the lies they have told about me.**

5. **That the Conservative Party, in return for the very large sums of money I have given them, should arrange for me to be given a life Dukedom in the style of the Duke of Del Monte, Earl Polly of Peck, Viscount Nadir of Asshole, Baron Maxwell.**

Conditions 6-10 have been placed in the Bank of North Cyprus and will not be revealed for 100 years.

THAT HISTORIC BOSNIAN PEACE PLAN IN FULL

(as signed by the USA, Russia and the EEC)

1. **The Serbs can do whatever they like.**
2. **Er…**
3. **That's it.**

DROPPING THE PILOT.

IL INDEPENDENTE

Edittore: Sgr Andreotti Whittamstrobini

2bn lira — FRIDAY, APRIL 23, 1993

Scandal taints entire Government

Can Majore Survive?

by Our Man in London ALESSANDRO CHANCELLORE

HAVING been in power as long as anyone can remember, the Non-Christian Non-Democrat Party (known as I Tories) was last night facing complete collapse as yet more names of top ministers were added to the ever-lengthening roll call of shame.

The embattled party leader Giovanni Majore, once widely respected by several of his Cabinet colleagues, now seems totally discredited, as he presides over what has been described as "the most incompetent and corrupt bunch of self-serving nonentities in history".

Michelangelo Heseltini, 60. Millionaire businessman caught out trying to "do a Maxwell" on Coal Board pension fund.

Vasco da Gumma, 52. Accepted free "pond" from agri-businessmen who hoped to benefit from EC regulations.

One by one they stand accused

Normanno Lamonte, 51. Accused of squandering billions of pounds of taxpayers' money in mad foreign exchange gambles. Also central figure in both the Onanugu and Miss Whiplash affairs. Used public money to hire notorious lawyer Pietro della Cartero Fucchini to threaten journalists.

Normanno di Fowleri, 54. Chairman of Non-Christian Non-Democratic Party. Now heavily implicated in the privatisation of prisons scandal (or "Opengate"). Openly admitted that he was "spending time with The Family".

Davide Mellore, 43. Forced to resign last year after he had been linked with Porn Queen Antonia di Pizza. Accepted swanky foreign holidays from wealthy Arab businessman.

La Signorina Thatcherina, 84. Known as "The Grandmother". For years she was the undisputed boss (or "Capo di Cino") of a gang of shady operators, ranging from the notorious Lord King to the absurd Lord Young. Her son Marco made millions out of alleged "deals" with Middle Eastern potentates.

Tristan Garel-Jones, 41. Kenneth Clarke, 44. Malcolm Rifkind, 46. The so-called "Matrix Churchill Three", who attempted to imprison innocent businessmen to cover up their own arms-dealing with Saddam Hussein.

Il Conte di Asshole, 52. Close intimate of both "The Grandmother" and Majore, Asshole throws lavish parties in his penthouse, serving "shepherd's pizzas" to the rich and powerful. Uses fiction-writing as a front to conceal the fact that he is one of the country's biggest twits (surely 'most influential men'? Ed.)